Kerry

'Kerry is mountain and ocean with a little bit of land in between,'
writes Des Lavelle, with typical Kerry understatement.
It is more. A wonderworld of stark beauty, of picturesque lakes,
a world full of woodland, lakeside, rivers, mountain,
and the ever-present stunning coastline pointing towards islands
alive with history and wildlife. Kerry is peopled by a race apart.
It is often windswept and misty, often sunladen,
but always beautiful, always welcoming.

"kerry"

text
DES LAVELLE

pictures
RICHARD HAUGHTON

THE O'BRIEN PRESS

First published 1986 by The O'Brien Press
20 Victoria Road, Rathgar, Dublin 6

British Library Cataloguing in Publication Data
Lavelle, Des
    Kerry.
    1. Kerry (Ireland) — Description and travel
    I. Title   II. Haughton, R.
    914.19'604824   DA990.K4
    ISBN 0-86278-086-1

10   9   8   7   6   5   4   3   2   1

Acknowledgements
For black-and-white photographs we wish to acknowledge the following:
Bord Fáilte pp 21, 22 bottom, 26, 27, 30, 39, 47, 53; Office of Public Works
pp 16, 20, 22 top, 38 top and bottom, 46, 49; George Gmelch pp 56, 69;
Richard Mills pp 61, 65 top and bottom; Des Lavelle pp 62 (colour), 68.

Book and cover design: Michael O'Brien
Edited by: Íde ní Laoghaire
Maps: Adrian Slattery
Typesetting: Phototype-Set Ltd., Dublin
Printing: Brough, Cox and Dunn Ltd., Belfast

Cover picture: Looking towards the Iveragh Peninsula from Inch Strand.

Page 2: Lough Gal, looking towards Slievenagower and Stradbally mountain.

Contents

A still ribbon of water flows into Ballyheige Bay in north Kerry.

The Magic of Kerry

Few explorers today are faced with the task – be it terrifying or exhilarating – of facing blindly into a new and uncharted destination. All countries, counties and villages have their own advance brochures. But they do not tell you much.

The other extreme is equally unsatisfactory – to delve deeply into every conceivable morsel of publication and eventually be so confused by an overabundance of information that nothing is left for the live performance. No longer can such explorers see with their own eyes the visual explosions around them, hear with their own ears the enchanting music on every side, or feel with their own senses the magical touch of one soul upon another.

In *Kerry* we try only to whet the appetite, and we trust that the Kerry you eventually search out and find will be your own, own, own ......

Kerry is mountain and ocean with a little bit of land in between. And of that land much is furze bush, rock and bog. Yet Kerry's praises are many and are sung daily in numerous languages. Perhaps this in itself proves one great truth: whatever aspect you look at – be it ogham stones, orchids or ornithology – Kerry's quota is invariably more impressive than that of any of its thirty-one neighbouring counties.

Yet, who can identify that elusive Kerry magnetism? The all-seeing eye of Richard Hayward would pinpoint his favourite facet: 'That wonderland of mountain, lake and majestic seaboard.' Synge would be more melodramatic, of course, and see in Kerry 'the desolation that is mixed everywhere with the supreme beauty of the world.'

But scenery and physical things are only part of the story; modern writers would lay the emphasis in a different sector. John B. Keane would say that the magic is in the people. 'The people of Kerry are larger than life. It is imperative that this be made clear from the outset!' And Brendan Kennelly would find his pleasure in the language of the people: 'The Kerry I cherish most is not the Kerry of landscape, glorious and varied though it may be, but the Kerry of language, song, story and personality.'

Perhaps this is getting nearer to the truth, for in Kerry, legends and folktales which had already survived for thousands of years before ever being committed to writing, are certainly as valuable a part of the heritage as any of the more cold proven facts of today. Indeed, in this county, legend and history blend so well together that it would be a very brave – or a very foolish – person who would seek to define the distinguishing line between them.

The same ancient storytelling

A relaxed moment at Cloghane sheep fair, on the Dingle Peninsula.

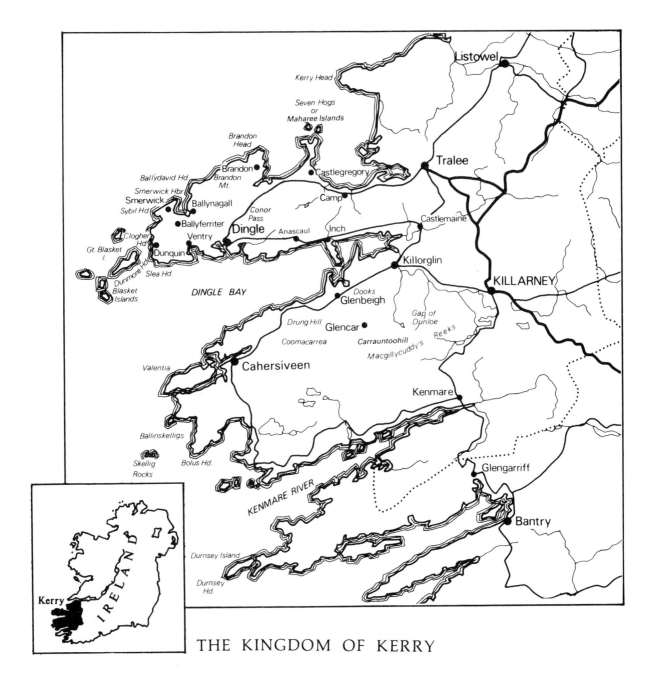

THE KINGDOM OF KERRY

art which handed down tale after precise tale still survives in Kerry today, albeit in a perverse, but no less skilful, way. For in Kerry – known as 'The Kingdom' perhaps because of its citizens' propensity to manage their own affairs of commerce, love, justice and retribution since time immemorial with much overt disregard for the dictates of central government, be that in Tara, London, Dublin or Brussels – the telling of outrageous lies is still a Kerryman's prerogative and duty.

Not for any motives of malice! No, indeed, but for the sheer, unadulterated pleasure of launching some monstrous disinformation on the entertainment circuit, in the full knowledge that each subsequent retelling will add and subtract so many embellishments as to render the original gem totally unrecognisable by the time it returns to its creator.

And how can the Kerryman, living in one of the poorest counties, attain the lightness of spirit necessary to become a champion warrior, champion athlete or champion prankster?

It is a simple philosophy: the Kerryman's back is to the mountain, and the ocean has already encroached as far as his knees. There is no retreat, no room for manoeuvre. And to shed tears for that fate would only make the ocean deeper. Life is now; it must be lived fully before the real flood comes!

A poor county indeed, but nevertheless a place where unbolted and open doors attract only fresh air, friendship and informality – something not easily understood by civilisations which stipulate three chains on every door and two shotguns under every bed! Behind the times, perhaps, but who wants to be up-to-date if the selling price is privacy and freedom?

The one catch in this incredible aspect of Kerry is that the native may not always see the wood for the trees. Therefore Kerry is also a place to get out of occasionally — if only for the sole purpose of appreciating its value all the more when one hurries home to its sanctuary.

Climate

Kerry is a bizarre place, behind time in a real sense, for here, in this most westerly land of Europe, the mean time of Greenwich in winter is out of phase with the reality of Kerry by forty minutes, and the British Summer Time of summer is one hour and forty minutes adrift! Yet, surprisingly, nobody has yet used this most logical Kerry argument to index Kerry pub-closing time to Kerry sun-time rather than to an imaginary line in the middle of a distant London suburb.

But even if Kerry Kingdom Time will never be official, at least it serves to create the benign hallucination that there are twenty-five hours in every Kerry day, allowing Kerryman and visitor alike to enjoy Kerry life at a slightly slower pace, and enabling those glorious midsummer Atlantic sunsets to go on and on until eleven o'clock at night.

Provided you can see the sunset, that is. For Kerry is a place of unique climate, too, and for all outdoor activities this must be taken into account – from day to day, and from one hour to the next.

Lying in the direct path of the prevailing south-westerly winds coming in off the Atlantic ocean, Kerry is the first county to have 'the weather', be it good news, or bad. First the bad news: sea breezes and high mountains are bad bedfellows, because warm, moist air rising to meet cold mountaintop results in cloud, mist and rain — and Kerry gets its fair share of these! Similarly, winter gales from the south-west will exert and expend much of their violence on Kerry before moving on and treating the areas inland less severely. But fortune was thoughtful too in building the Kerry coast of durable old red sandstone cliffs which have successfully battled the Atlantic for thousands of years. Wounded, perhaps; scarred, yes indeed; but still standing and prepared to slog it out for ever.

A dreadful climate? A stormlashed existence? Notwithstanding such awesome possibilities, that eminent, unbiased scholar, botanist and traveller, Robert Lloyd Praeger, wrote: 'I have not had more soakings in Kerry than elsewhere in Ireland, and, indeed, on two

Cirrus clouds, indicating a thundery tendency, over Kenmare's environs.

found in the bogland, lakeland and valley habitats of Kerry.

A Kerryman must not be asked to decide whether the weather should be boasted about, apologised for, or completely falsified, so a brief table of statistics is the best answer. It bares the soul adequately, yet provides the off-chance that the reader will see only the favourable assets!

So it blows? So it rains? Soon the wind will veer north-west and moderate, the rain will change to showers, the sun will come out and Kerry will be treated to that special, exclusive, inexplicably clear light so beloved of artists and photographers.

All will be forgiven!

occasions work was impeded by heat and drought!'

Heat and drought? A look at the other side – the good news – of Kerry's climate may explain that. The warm Gulf Stream, with its equatorial and Bahamian components, in Kerry's surrounding Atlantic is a very real influence, and to this can be attributed a general mildness of climate over the whole county. Kerry's long rocky toes reach out to this great hot-water bottle and salvage enough warmth to keep the mean minimum winter air temperature as high as five degrees centigrade. Frost and ice are seldom a problem here and snow is rare, even on higher ground. Consequently, early agricultural crops and natural flora are generally more advanced

in Kerry than in other counties. Indeed, quite a number of wildflower species which more properly would be at home in Spain or Portugal are commonly

Driest month:	May – 83.5mm (3.3in.) rainfall
Wettest month:	December – 167mm (6.6in.) rainfall
Mean annual rainfall:	1412mm (55.6in.) rainfall
Hottest months:	July and August – mean daily minimum: 13°C; mean daily maximum: 18°C
Coldest month:	February – mean daily minimum: 5°C; mean daily maximum: 9°C
Air frost:	Number of days per year – (0°C or lower): 10
Temperature:	Extreme values – 27°C to -7°C
Windiest month:	December – average midday wind speed: 13kn;
Maximum winter gust:	83kn
Calmest months:	July and August – average midday wind speed: 10kn

Altocumulus clouds, indicating light winds at cloud level, form stunning patterns over the Dingle Peninsula.

Origins

The story of this land is old, much older than the year 1606 when the modern boundaries of the county took shape. It dates from no less than four hundred million years ago.

The stuff that Kerry is made of was first laid down in those dim ages when most of Ireland rose from the sea and became part of a high continental desert. Sun and torrential rains caused great piles of sand to accumulate on the ocean floor, where endless time and immense pressure cemented them into great solid rock layers. The ancient seas receded, and later returned, and this time a different debris of softer, lime-rich material built further layer upon rock layer. A hundred million years passed and other pressures playing within the earth's crust buckled these rock layers violently, forcing mighty ridges upwards and deep valleys downwards. Outflows of lava occurred, giving rise to Kerry's volcanic exceptions like Clogher Head in the Dingle Peninsula. Local pressure points created such geological oddities as the once-quarried Killarney marble or the well-known Kerry 'diamonds' – those pretty, if worthless, gems of white, blue or clear silica dioxide quartz. Deposits of copper became lodged at Muckross and Ross Island in Killarney and at Caherdaniel's Coad Mountain; soft deposits of chalk or white

limestone survived at Brennan's Glen near Killarney. But sun, wind, rain and ploughing ice for a million years stripped the Kerry peaks of every vestige of softer materials and the remainder became the fleshless, craggy bones of Kerry – a monument in old red sandstone.

Old? Yes, indeed. Red? Not necessarily, but commonly green, yellow or purple. Sand-like? Never. But as tough as any stone in Ireland, yet sculpted, shaped and scattered by what so often looks like the wanton play of glaciers.

8500 B.C. experienced a sudden warming of climate. Plant life became possible and forests took a firm hold, forests which were the direct ancestors of the now rare native oakwoods of Kerry – at Muckross National Park, Tomies Wood, Derrycunnihy Wood and Camillan Wood (all near Killarney), and at Uragh Wood near Kenmare.

By 5000 B.C. sea level had risen by one hundred metres, flooding the lowland connections with Britain and making Ireland into an island. The Atlantic filled Kerry's long bays, putting nature's basic shape to some 1,161,700 acres (470,133 hectares) of 'The Kingdom'.

Two kingdoms really, in the geological sense: the mountainous old red sandstone of the south and west being synonymous with poor soil; the carboniferous limestone of the north Kerry lowlands generally indicating good, fertile land, and the dividing line between the two being clearly visible today at Killarney's

lakeside. On one shore stand the old red sandstone peaks, while on the other shore are beautiful examples of age-old but ongoing erosion in soft limestone caverns.

So, from 8000 B.C. Kerry had an environment fit for man. It would be perhaps another five thousand years before we would claim it.

HUMAN HABITATION

If Palaeolithic or Early Stone Age man of about 8000 B.C. ever came to Kerry, we have no traces of them. But Kerry was no stranger to other early visitors, and Mesolithic man of perhaps 5000 B.C. may have been involved in the habitation of sandhill sites near Inch strand, Castlegregory and Ballybunion, where the diet included shellfish and bear — if finds of discarded shells and a bear's tooth are adequate proof. Current radio-carbon dating of archaeological finds at Ferriter's Cove, at the tip of the Dingle Peninsula, indicate a Neolithic settlement there of about 3500 B.C. There are major marks in Kerry of habitation from 3000 B.C. in the shape of megalithic burial sites, standing stones, stone circles and dolmens, bearing a conspicuous resemblance to megalithic remains on the coast of Brittany.

But it was the Bronze Age citizens from 2000 B.C. who left us the most remarkable number of splendid remains. No longer specialising only in stone burial chambers, they produced fine craftsmanship in copper, bronze and gold. One hoard of copper weapons and tools from Killaha East, near Kenmare, contained a copper dagger of unusual shape, similar to a find dated 1935 B.C. from Newgrange. Knockasarnet, near Killarney, yielded other similar treasures. One find in about A.D. 1936 was a Bronze Age bowl which was still in use for feeding chickens!

They left us more. A Celtic language — perhaps from 1000 B.C., though not in any written form for such would not appear until about A.D. 500 as ogham inscriptions — but a basic language root which later became the Irish language.

LEGEND

Longside the more serious and scholarly studies of the archaeologists, the early history of Kerry's inhabitants comes to us through legend, which puts names on the various groups that landed on the coast and credits them with exotic and fanciful activities. Through the tradition of storytelling these colourful 'facts' were handed down from generation to generation, but the first written account is contained in the *Book of Invasions,* written in the Middle Ages.

The stories tell of the occupation of Ireland by the Fomorians and the Fir Bolg peoples, and by that godlike race, the Tuatha dé Danann, who were reputed to use magic to sort out any difficulties - such as invaders - that threatened them. They also tell of various invasions said to have occurred in the Kerry region.

'Forty days before the Deluge,' according to the stories, and referring to the Great Flood, 'Ceasair came to Ireland with fifty girls and three men; Bith, Ladhra and Fintain their names . . .' Ceasair was the grand-daughter of Noah, who refused to allow her into the Ark, and hers was the only ship of the expedition to make a safe landing in Ballinskelligs Bay as the two other vessels and their crews had been lost. Clearly there were no virile Kerrymen in that south-western barony of Iveragh at the time; the fifty women were divided between the three men, a duty that was to cost two of the men their lives, and the other his sanity! (*See Ring of Kerry section.*)

Three hundred years later, Parthalon, who was fleeing from Greece after murdering his parents, landed with a thousand followers at Lamb's Head in Kenmare Bay. But his sanctuary was shortlived; the one-eyed Balor and his Fomorian demons made life unbearable for the new arrivals, and eventually a plague wiped out the Parthalonian tribe in a matter of nine days.

Next came the fleet of Milesius with his sons Ir and Amergin – and a peculiar complement of forty-eight married couples and four mercenary soldiers! Hardly an invasion force in itself, and possibly more concerned with commercial considerations of the copper deposits on the shores of Kenmare Estuary. But they had a difficult time too. Scéne, wife of Amergin, died at sea in Kenmare Estuary (to which she gave her name, *Inbhear Scéine*) and Ir also died on board ship and was buried at Skellig. There were other fatalities, and even those who landed safely at Waterville still had to contend with the wiles of the local tribe of the Tuatha dé Danann, who had control of all Ireland. The Tuatha de Danann persuaded the Milesians to move back out to sea until the local chieftain, as a matter of courtesy, could be informed of their arrival! But, of course, as soon as the Milesians complied, a magical storm conjured up by the Tuatha dé Danann wrecked yet another of the fleet, drowning its crew and its captain, Donn, at the Bull Rock, known ever since as Teach Duinn (Donn' house).

But the Tuatha dé Danann paid sorely for their treachery; when the storm abated the Milesians eventually came ashore in force and went on the rampage through the county and through the country, where they beat all that came before them, forced the Tuatha dé Danann to a preternatural existence underground, and stayed on, settled in Kerry and very soon began calling themselves Kerrymen.

Some of the more tangible early Kerrymen of folklore vintage from about A.D. 200 were the Fianna, mercenaries who for fame or principle or chivalry would espouse a cause and wage war against all odds under their leader – champion and folk hero, Fionn MacCumhail. Fionn's exploits were wide-ranging, and to steal the wife and daughter of the King of France was all in a day's work! But such deeds eventually incurred the wrath of the King of

Left: Gallans (standing stones) at Cloonsharragh – the stones are orientated towards the summit of Mount Brandon.

Right: Inbhear Scéine (Kenmare Bay), named after Scéne, one of the Milesian invaders of ancient legend.

the World, and the subsequent battle of a year-and-a-day at Ventry Strand was almost the undoing of Fionn. Undaunted, however, he was in action again shortly afterwards, this time at Ballybunion, allegedly defending the daughter of the King of Greece from her husband! One thousand of the Fianna died for that cause but they eventually won the day!

Fionn's life was one successful rout after another, and rather late in years – when he should have known better – he got rather exalted ideas and precipitated a complex love triangle by deciding to marry Gráinne, daughter of the King of Ireland! (*See Ring of Kerry section – Glenbeigh.*)

A Glance at History

For some of the more concrete facts from the Christian period in Kerry nobody has to look further than the exciting *Annals of Inisfallen* (Ed. Seán Mac Airt) to read the whole truth.

The original of this manuscript, now retained in the Bodleian Library, Oxford, was compiled about the year A.D. 1092 and probably included earlier documents from the monastery of Emly, Co. Tipperary, as well as

the contemporary history written at the island monastery of Inisfallen in Killarney's Lough Leane, reporting all the relevant happenings to 1326, with later additions to 1450.

One entry, for example, tells of the Viking raids on the Kerry coast: 'A.D. 824. Scelec [Skellig] was plundered by the heathens and Étgal was carried off into captivity, and he died of hunger on their hands.' Behind this stark headline we can visualise an era of ninth-century terror in the Kerry coastal communities as the Norsemen in their sleek longships probed Kerry's bays and estuaries, plundering and robbing en route with scant respect for layman, churchman — or life itself.

Another entry in the *Annals* tells how the manuscripts themselves later escaped destruction, not by the Vikings but by an equally ferocious Irish plunderer:

'A.D. 1180. There was committed in this year a deed which greatly vexed the clergy of all Ireland, namely the plundering of Inis Faithlinn by Mael Duin, son of Donall Ua Donnchada, and the carrying off by him of all the worldly wealth therein, which was under the protection of its saints, clerics and consecrated churches. He collected, indeed, the gold, silver, trappings, mantles, and cloaks of Iarmumu, without any respect for God or man, but the mercy of God did not allow him to kill people or to strip this heavenly place of church furnishings or books.'

DISPOSSESSION

It was easy – and fashionable – to pillage monasteries in the twelfth century. The Normans by comparison, whose invasion of Kerry began in A.D. 1200 and who had the benefit of archery, calvary and armour, did not find conquest of Kerry so easy and took nearly three hundred years to master the entire county! North Kerry and the Dingle Peninsula readily came under the Anglo-Norman influence of the Geraldine Earl of Desmond, but in the mountainous south the Gaelic way of life continued almost uninterrupted under the Gaelic King of Desmond — McCarthy, later called McCarthy More (from *mór* meaning 'big').

Today a still-visible chain of now-ruined castles along the valleys of the rivers Maine, Laune and Roughty marks the east-west boundary across the centre of the county which separated Kerry's coexisting Anglo-Norman and Gaelic worlds for nearly four centuries. However, in the 1650s the Cromwellian forces finally brought the English invasion in its more violent form to the far reaches of the Iveragh Peninsula. Dispossession, eviction, removal, confiscation of land were suddenly the order of the day under a Statute passed in August 1652. The dispossessed O'Connell family of Iveragh, for example, was banished to county Clare; the O'Connor lands at Carrigafoyle

were granted to a Cromwellian settler named Sandes. And in the juggling with lives and properties one arch-gangster emerged with almost a quarter of Kerry in his private possession! He was Dr – later Sir – William Petty, a doctor with the invading forces, who expedited the dispossessions and evictions by speedily and efficiently mapping out the properties, receiving for himself in grants and cheap acquisitions some 270,000 acres (111,709 hectares) of the county.

LEARNING

But if Kerrymen lost land, possessions and freedom in this

harsh era, there was still one aspect of Kerry character which neither edict nor fear of reprisal could suppress – the hunger for knowledge, books and education which were always part of the Kerry spirit. 'Going to Kerry for learning' was a reality of the time as students congregated illicitly at the Kerry hedge-schools for wide-ranging studies, studies which, despite the difficulties of the situation, were real enough to draw comment at the time. Sir William Petty himself (c.1672) mentioned that though the Irish were living 'in a brutish nasty Condition, as in Cabins, with neither Door, Stairs nor Window' a knowledge of the French and Latin tongues was 'very frequent amongst the poorer Irish and chiefly in Kerry'. Lord Herbert's report of 1673, entitled 'A mode for better regulating the County' (of Kerry), confirmed, but hardly appreciated, such achievements: 'The said county aboundeth,' he observed, 'with youth learning of needless latin instead of useful trades'.

POETS

In that seventeenth century also the early Kerry poets came upon the scene – that much-mentioned quartet of Piaras Feiritéar, Geoffrey O'Donoghue, Aogán Ó Rathaille and Eoghan Rua Ó Súilleabháin.

Piaras Feiritéar (c.1600-1653) was a chieftain from the Dingle Peninsula, and the remnants of his power-base, Ferriter's Castle, are still in existence today near Ferriter's Cove. He was well known in high society, and even wrote love poems to Meg Russell, a relative of the Queen's viceroy in Ireland. But Feiritéar was also a champion of the poorer people, and despite his Norman descent he threw in his support with the native Irish, leading the siege of Tralee Castle in 1641. His lot thus cast, the ultimate outcome was inevitable – Piaras Feiritéar, soldier, chieftain, poet in the Irish language, was hanged publicly by the Cromwellians at Killarney in 1653, and thus gained the status of folk hero, which status he still holds today in the Gaeltacht of Corca Dhuibhne, the Dingle Peninsula.

Geoffrey O'Donoghue (c.1620-1678) of Killaha, Glenflesk (near Killarney), was also involved in the siege of Tralee Castle in 1641, but the Cromwellians did not attempt any subsequent vengeance against him and he continued to live his wild, jolly life, becoming better known for his extravagant parties at his tower house than for his warring potential. O'Donoghue's verse was much appreciated in his own time, but is little known today.

Aogán Ó Rathaille (c.1675-1792) was born to reasonably prosperous parents in the Sliabh Luachra region of east Kerry, and had a good schooling in Latin, English, Irish literature and history. But when O'Rathaille's benefactor, Sir Nicholas Browne, lost his lands through confiscation in 1690, O'Rathaille was forced to leave his comfortable circumstances and live in unaccustomed hardship – part wanderer, part resident – in the vicinity of Castlemaine harbour, a step he was to bemoan in his poetry.

But it was the sight of destruction all around him, the fall of the great families who were once his home-from-home, the treachery and deceit, and the sight of his own people abandoning their religion and joining the enemy for the sake of power, that finally evoked O'Rathaille's most sombre litany of woe and sorrow – so dreary and so monotonous that it fully conveys O'Rathaille's wretched feelings.

Eoghan Rua Ó Súilleabháin (1748-1784) was born in the same Sliabh Luachra area as Ó Rathaille, but there the similarity ends. Ó Súilleabháin, wit and playboy, was a schoolmaster at the age of eighteen, promiscuous *spailpín* (wandering) labourer at twenty, sailor in the British navy, and, still only in his thirties, discontented soldier in the British army!

Typical of Eoghan Rua's style was a poem he wrote as soon as he finally – through self-inflicted injury – got out of the army. He returned to Kerry to set up a school and addressed the following to Fr Ned Fitzgerald, parish priest of Eoghan Rua's birthplace:

Reverend Sir –
Please publish from the altar of your holy Mass
That I will open school at Knocknagree Cross,
Where the tender babes will be well off,

The Iveragh Peninsula with Inch Strand in the foreground.

Lough Leane, Killarney, with Carrauntoohil in the background. It was here on the island of Inisfallen that the Annals of Innisfallen were written.

For it's there I'll teach them their Criss Cross ...
With all young ladies I'll engage
To forward them with speed and care,
With book-keeping and mensuration,
Euclid's Elements and Navigation ...
With the grown-up youths I'll first agree

To instruct them well in the Rule of Three;
Such of them as are well able,
The Cube root of me will learn,
Such as are of a tractable genius,
With compass and rule I will teach them,
Bills, bonds and informations ...
And sweet love letters for the ladies.

The school did not last long, and neither did Eoghan Rua. An ale-house injury in Killarney – allegedly a blow on the head with a pair of tongs – was the beginning of the end, and shortly afterwards Eoghan Rua Ó Súilleabháin, poet in two languages, died at thirty-six years of age.

But he had one last jest at the

world before he joined his people and his fellow poets in Muckross Abbey: due to floods on the Blackwater river, his funeral cortège could not reach Killarney, so he was temporarily buried at Nohavile until the floods subsided — and thus started one more argument: '... even to this day,' says Daniel Corkery's *The Hidden Ireland* (1924), 'some of the people of that countryside assert that the poet lies at Nohavile [nowadays Nohaval], where the original grave was dug.' The debate continues. The truculent poet would have been pleased!

FACTION FIGHTS

Life in Gaelic Ireland was not totally a matter of poetry, word-play and lament, however. No perusal of Kerry's past can omit the wild faction fights that were so much part of everyday life up to the nineteenth century (and sometimes later). These violent feuds, which may have sprung from something as simple as an inter-family squabble, soon involved village versus village and townland versus townland, and went on through generations until the participants had no idea what the original argument was about. Some admitted, or boasted, that the only reason they were fighting was because their fathers and grandfathers had fought before them.

Some of these faction fights were annual events, such as 15 August at Knockanure or 13 December at Tralee, but others continued intermittently from one fair-day or market-day to the

next, when alcohol, even if it was not the cause of the flames, was good fuel for them. Recurrent showdowns included those between the Dillanes and the Sheehys of Duagh, the Brosnans and the O'Connors of Castleisland, the Moynihans and O'Donoghues of Killarney. The vicinities of Tralee, Kenmare, Dingle, Ardfert, Killorglin and Listowel all knew localised encounters, where heads were split, blood spilled, bones broken, and sometimes a life – or two, or three – lost. But the classic of all faction fights was that between the Cooleens and the Mulvihills – a long-standing, bitter feud, which kept the three north Kerry baronies of Clanmaurice, Iraghticonnor and Trughanacmy in turmoil for forty years, from 1794 to 1834!

This feud was to bring faction fighting to a climax on 24 June 1834 at the horse races on Ballagh strand, on the banks of the Cashen river, near Ballybunion. The race programme was never completed that day. Instead, some 1,500 Mulvihills and 1,000 Cooleens fell upon one another. Amidst a war of such proportions, thirteen police and sixty soldiers were powerless to keep the peace. The battle went badly for the Cooleens. They were beaten back into the river and the boatloads of stones and missiles which they themselves had gathered for the fray now rained down on their own heads!

Reports of the carnage vary. H.D. Inglis said: 'Nearly two score persons were driven into the Shannon and drowned and

knocked on the head like so many dogs.' Samuel Lewis reported that 'sixteen were killed or drowned while endeavouring to cross the Cashen ferry', and a police report of July 1834 mentioned that fifteen bodies had been recovered from the river, and that two were still missing.

Large-scale faction fights were never the same again, and today the slow, sluggish Cashen river still flows seaward, a paradoxical monument to the high, flushed tempers of north Kerry.

Dunloe ogham stone (near Killarney), clearly showing the inscription in this ancient form of writing.

Monuments

Ardfert, one of north Kerry's most splendid monuments.

Kerry has sixty-eight designated national monuments, and these are only the sixty-eight major items. The thousands of other archaeological and historical sites in the county will probably defy forever our efforts to count, catalogue and explore them as more items, more settlements, more remains show up each year.

Unfortunately, the number of monuments of yesterday obliterated from the face of the earth by agricultural and other developments is too numerous to count. And to compound the sin many such sites had never been investigated and whatever archaeological significance they may have had has disappeared with them. Once upon a time it was traditional to respect, or perhaps fear, those traces of ancient habitation – the 'fairy fort' supposedly inhabited by the 'little people' but in truth the remains of the dwelling places of our ancient ancestors. The mythology protecting such sacred sites for centuries died with the advent of the 'Bulldozer Age' which put paid to such traditional hangups and wiped out some 44 percent of the county's archaeological earthworks in one novel swoop. Perhaps this particular rot has stopped now. Perhaps landowners are more aware of the importance of things ancient. Perhaps.

Kerry has an abundance of ogham stones, standing slabs bearing memorial inscriptions in ogham script which date from about A.D. 500. Of three hundred ogham stones in Ireland Kerry has 121, and of these some seventy are packed into Corca Dhuibhne (the Dingle Peninsula) alone.

But how many of them stand in their original sites? Lord Ventry, in the mid-nineteenth century, had a habit of digging them up and presenting them to his relations at Chute Hall, near Tralee, or standing them in the vicinity of his own property at Burnham, Dingle! In fact the ogham stone at Emlagh East (near Dingle) – the first to be deciphered in Ireland – has been to Chute Hall and back. Other ogham stones have travelled too. The eight Dunloe ogham stones (near Killarney), excellent examples of their kind, may look as though they have stood in the same circle for 1,400 years, but this is not so! Those forming the circle came to light in 1838 in part of the roof of nearby Coolmagort souterrain, and the centre stone came from the church at Kilbonane, several kilometres away. The Derrynane ogham stone was found 'below the water line' – presumably sea-level – and was re-erected on its present site. Another homeless ogham stone was placed at Ballywiheen (Ballyferriter) for safe-keeping, but it was broken in two before 1970. And one of seven ogham stones at Kilcoolaght East (Killarney) was stolen about 1960!

NORTH KERRY

Kerry is conspicuously two kingdoms in terms of archaeological remains, for while the south and the west of the county are top-heavy with monuments of prehistoric times, and are riddled with archaeological excavations and well-documented reports, north Kerry's known roots, with minimal exceptions, reach back only to the Christian period. Despite the discovery there of some ancient treasures – a bronze axe at Listowel, a dug-out canoe and three stone axe-heads at Dysert, a gold box and a bronze dagger at Ballinclemsig, a bronze bowl at Galey, and other items now in the National Museum – the north Kerry area has received relatively little official archaeological examination.

In fact, many of the stoneworks of north Kerry's archaeological sites made more history in their demolition, often by cannon and flames, than they did in their construction or rediscovery. The 1537 Statute for the Suppression of Abbeys sounded a death-knell for many church establishments and for many churchmen. Lislaughtin Friary, for instance,

Listowel Castle, from the Norman period, in north Kerry.

founded in 1478, saw three of its aged Franciscans murdered before the high altar on 6 April 1580. The disorder of the Elizabethan and Cromwellian wars witnessed the destruction of north Kerry's chain of fine castles – Ballybunion,

Ballykealy, Ballymacaquin, Beal, Carrigafoyle, Doon, Lick, Listowel, Lixnaw and Port. The end result of these wars was a trail of rather sad ruins, some, such as Ballybunion Castle, poignantly picturesque, but all with a pitiful, gruesome story, and all in such a state that – in stark comparison to the richness of south and west Kerry – only a handful of north Kerry sites are rated as national monuments today. These are: Ardfert cathedral, churches and friary; Carrigafoyle Castle; Chute Hall ogham stones; Lislaughtin Friary; Listowel Castle; Ratass Church, Tralee; Tonaknock stone cross, Lixnaw; Ratoo church and round tower.

But even if north Kerry has few physical remains from the Early Christian period, it certainly can be proud of its renowned human champion from that era, that patron of Kerry, mountain-top hermit and intrepid traveller, St Brendan.

The well-preserved round tower of Ratoo, near Ballyduff, in north Kerry.

*Gallarus Oratory,
the most perfect of the
Early Christian dry
rubble buildings in
Ireland (see p. 49).*

Travel

Almost deserving of national monument status are Kerry's roads! 'The worst in all Ireland, impassible in winter time, and requiring an hour's riding with much trouble and danger for each mile', said a critic in 1673, and latterday commentators are frequently equally unkind. But who wants a dull monotonous autobahn where more people die from counting sheep than from colliding with them? To what purpose a six-lane highway over the snake-like Ballaghisheen Pass, where it would only serve to make those twisted, tortured, tormented roadside holly trees and the ragged remnants of old oakwoods flash inconspicuously by like a soon-forgotten summer side-salad?

Kerry's winding roads impose their own appropriate speed limit, and since the shortest distance between two points is certainly not a straight line, the traveller has mandatory time to reflect on the multiple miracles: that so many inaccessible places merited roadways in the first instance; that so many negotiable levels were ever surveyed in such a mountainous maze; and that Kerry County Council manages to keep its 4,200km of public roadway functioning so well in such far-flung, varying territories and altitudes, from the 333 metre-high Healy Pass, connecting Cork and Kerry between Lauragh and

Adrigole, to the 416 metre-high Conor Pass, with its Kerry-to-Clare panoramas, between Dingle and Cloghane. Over rock and under it go Kerry's roads, near the Turner's Rock tunnels at 400 metres altitude between Kenmare and Glengarriff; over water and through it at Glenfahan Ford, near Slea Head; over long sections of trembling bog in every parish of the county, and even occasionally under salt water and storm-blown beach sand near Castlegregory!

It is little wonder that the earliest roads in Kerry came in by the easy, northern, coastal lowlands: Glin, Tarbert, Carrigafoyle, Listowel, Finuge, Lixnaw and Ardfert. Smith's *History of Kerry* in 1756 shows this line – and little else – but by 1845 travel conditions had so improved that the county surveyor could boast: 'Every horse now has his cart instead of his baskets.'

The current boast, as major roadworks progress, is that a car and a coach can now pass each other with safety over much of the Drung Hill section of the Ring of Kerry road. Road-widening work on this stretch of highway, which clings to the cliff face on the southern shore of Dingle Bay, is monumental indeed — tons of solid rock have been pared from the steep cliff face on the inshore side of the roadway and tipped over the slope on the seaward side, thus gaining a few precious metres on either side.

JARVEYS

The jarveys of Killarney town and

the many ponymen of the Gap of Dunloe have been part of the Kerry transport scene since tourism began and have featured in the standard 'holiday in Ireland' illustrations in even the oldest guides. And even today this mode of transport still enjoys a peculiarly priviledged position in the area, aided by the prohibition of motor cars in much of the Muckross National Park lakeland circuit, and the generally accepted belief that the Gap of Dunloe road is better suited to ponies than to Peugeots, Porsches and such! The scenery of the Gap can certainly be best enjoyed on horseback – letting the animal take care of the familiar potholes and the 180° hairpin bends, and letting the human attentions concentrate on the neck-breaking, vertical cliff scenes reaching up to the sky on either hand.

And having ventured this far, the half-way Gap trip is not enough. One should 'do' all 20km of it, from Kate Kearney's Cottage to the mouth of the Black Valley and then returning to Killarney by boat via the Upper Lake, the Long Range river, Muckross Lake and Lough Leane. It will take a whole day, and novice horsemen will need another day to recover from saddle fatigue!

RAILWAYS

For anyone who is a confirmed dreamer, Kerry railway stations are fascinating – not so much in their architecture, be it the cut stone of Killarney from 1853, the cut stone of Tralee from 1859, or

A blacksmith at work in Castleisland, north Kerry – once a familiar sight.

the corrugated iron huts of the Kenmare and Cahersiveen branch line from 1893; nor in the untimely closure with unseemly haste of those branches in 1960, dealing such a callous blow to the isolated communities of the south-west; nor in the fact that the peculiar Lartigue line which linked Listowel to Ballybunion, 1888-1924, was the only monorail train in these islands; nor in the great carnage when the Dingle to Tralee narrow-gauge train, 1891-1953, leapt off a viaduct near Camp in 1893, killing three men and ninety pigs; but in this fact of life – for many Kerry people the more important considerations than their roots in the county, were their routes out of it!

According to the census returns, Kerry's population in the post-Famine decade, dropped by 31 per cent (from 293,880 to 238,245) overall and by as much as 46 per cent in pockets of particular hardship such as Tuosist parish, Kenmare. The trend has continued in a downward spiral from 201,039 in 1881 to 112,772 in 1971.

Even the +6 per cent reprieve of 1979 which brought the county's population up to 120,356 was not uniformly reflected. The urban populations increased, some rural districts stabilised, but the extreme south-west – from Glenbeigh to Caherdaniel – continued in decline over the period 1971 to 1979 by –6.2%. The omens for the future are frightening.

To stand and dream in Killarney's windy railway station today, not on a holiday weekend

The jarvey, providing the common mode of transport in Muckross National Park, Killarney.

when busy comings and goings disguise the real facts, but in a quiet empty moment, and to stare out along the cold, steel tracks is to look into an empty, hungry grave, ready to claim more of Kerry's youth and strength and beauty. To hear a sinister whisper on the Tannoy – 'The train now standing at platform number one is bound for Dublin, Camden Town, the Bronx, San Francisco, Melbourne ... one-way tickets only' – is to realise that this 'gateway to Kerry' has seen more departures than arrivals. And if the poignant monuments to their going are cut stone or corrugated iron, it matters not.

The Ring of Kerry

What a pity that Killarney town, with its magnificent Pugin-designed cathedral and its quaint laneways, was not built on the lakeside of Lough Leane, and that the main route south-westward to Killorglin does not follow the high road near Aghadoe. For this, in one coup, would expose for everyone's appreciation the magnificent combination of lake and mountain scenery which now lies just beyond the traveller's grasp, and would take in the church and round tower at Aghadoe – national monuments which originated with a monastery founded by St Fionan the Leper in the seventh century. But then, perhaps, it is nice to know at the start of this scenery-laden journey that some of the best views remain just that little bit hidden, and must be hunted down.

Unless one is captivated and entertained by the remarkable growth of ivy which seems to transform the Killarney-Killorglin roadside telephone poles, making them into bushy – if wire-sprouting – trees, the traveller must be prepared to make detours from the main road in this section of the Ring for items of interest.

Ballymalis Castle, 13km from Killarney, is one such detour. One of the first castles built by the Anglo-Normans in the thirteenth century, the present-day building is largely a sixteenth-century construction built by the Ferris family who were guardians of this section of the Laune river.

KILLORGLIN

Killorglin town, attractively situated on the Laune, grew up around Castle Conway (or Killorglin Castle), a thirteenth-century advance post of the Fitzgeralds. The castle is almost entirely ruined, and Killorglin is better known nowadays for its remarkable three-day horse and cattle fair, Puck Fair, held annually on 10-12 August. On the first day of the fair, Gathering Day, a large male goat (puck) – allegedly captured wild from a mountain herd – is decked out in ribbons and led through the town, crowned King of the Fair and raised on a pedestal high above the square, from where he presides over the business and the merrymaking of the fair below. It is argued that this tradition stems from Norman times when, in many parts of Europe, an animal was customarily displayed over a town to announce that a fair was in progress. But perhaps a more interesting suggestion is that Puck Fair's goat symbol, traditionally a symbol of fertility and licentiousness, derives its origin from a pagan festival worshipping the Celtic god Lug, who is

Killorglin, home of Puck Fair, nestling in the hills above the Laune river.

Looking out over Lough Leane at Ross Castle, Killarney.

region. The combination of lake, colour and brooding mountains constitute one of the finest inland views in Kerry.

GLENBEIGH

Glenbeigh village is on the main road, and as a holiday resort is well situated within striking distance of Rossbeigh sands at the head of Dingle Bay, and of the splendid fishing rivers, lakes and streams of the Caragh system. Glenbeigh's most famous historical landmark is the ruin of Winn's Folly (or Glenbeigh Towers), an elaborate dwelling from 1870 which was burned in 1922. This building is a monument to the eccentricity and extravagance of its owner, the fourth Baron Headley-Winn, and equally a monument to the incompetence of its architect, W.E. Godwin, who spent so much time entertaining the famous actress Ellen Terry during the construction that he was sued by Headley for excessive costs – as well as for leaking roofs and walls! Perhaps Headley may be forgiven in Glenbeigh for applying the rigours of the law in that case, but his name is more frequently remembered for the notorious Glenbeigh evictions of 1866-7 and for his excessive use of force against unfortunate local tenants who had rent arrears.

But Glenbeigh has older tales, and from the folklore of this area comes the well-known story of the pursuit of Diarmuid and Gráinne. Gráinne was the daughter of the King of Ireland – in the misty past – and was

commemorated in many places in the area.

Caragh Lake is another detour

from the Ring road, and it scarcely matters which approach one takes to this tree-covered, flower-filled

Galloping over the Kerry sands to Tír na nÓg!

Winn's Folly, Glenbeigh, a monument to eccentricity, extravagance and incompetence.

betrothed to Fionn MacCumhail, the leader of the famous Fianna. Gráinne did not want to marry Fionn and would have preferred his son, Oisin, instead. He, however, did not take up the offer, and thus she eloped with Diarmuid Ó Duibhne, the son of the King of Corca Dhuibhne (the Dingle Peninsula) instead.

According to the story the pair hid in a cave at Glenbeigh, but Fionn pursued them and they had to flee. They spent the next seven years chasing — and being chased — from pillar to post and from dolmen to cave to cliff. Finally, a truce was agreed between the warring factions. But, truce or not, Fionn finally had his way and managed to arrange for a wild boar to do away with Diarmuid on the slopes of Ben Bulbin (Co. Sligo) and thus clear the way for his much-delayed wedding to Gráinne!

Rossbeigh beach, only a 1km detour from the main Glenbeigh-Cahersiveen road, features in another well-known legend of the same period. This is the story of Oisin (the son of Fionn MacCumhail) and the beautiful, golden haired Niamh. Niamh invited Oisin to go with her to her home in Tír na nÓg, the land of perpetual youth. He agreed, and they galloped away on a white horse over the waves at Rossbeigh beach to Tír na nÓg where they lived for what (unknown to Oisin) was three hundred years.

But Oisin became restless. He wanted to see his old home and his friends again. So, mounted on the white horse, and warned by Niamh not to dismount under any circumstances, he galloped back over the sea at Rossbeigh and on to the old hunting grounds near Glencar, to a place now called Ballaghisheen (Oisin's Gap). However, he could find no trace of the Fianna. He searched throughout the country and went as far as the borders of Meath. There he saw some men moving boulders in a slow and laborious fashion. So shocked was Oisin by their feeble performance that he reached down from his horse to assist them. Then the girth broke and Oisin's feet touched the ground. Immediately, Oisin became an old, old man. Alone, the white horse galloped away, back to the golden-haired Niamh beyond the white waves of Rossbeigh.

At Mountain Stage the road reaches for its first sea view. This place brings memories of J.M. Synge, whose well-known, laconic essays on Kerry were written here. Drung Hill, reputedly the burial place of St Fionan, that major founding figure of many south Kerry religious establishments, dominates the scenery on one hand, and Dingle Bay suddenly dominates on the other. Distractions are few here, unless one has the inclination to decipher the painted and overpainted political slogans which much detract from the stark architectural beauty of the stone-built railway viaduct at Gleensk, where the disused railway and the Ring road cling equally perilously to the cliff face before guiding the traveller to the safer terrain surrounding the next picturesque detour to the sand and sea at Kells Bay.

CARHAN AND CAHERSIVEEN

Carhan, on the eastern outskirts of Cahersiveen, rests on its laurels as the birthplace of Daniel O'Connell, that most famous of all Irishmen. The 'Liberator', as he was known, studied in France and in London, and as well as becoming a most successful lawyer was also the engineer of Irish democracy and of Catholic Emancipation in 1829. O'Connell's birthplace was humble, and in its present ruined state looks even more so, but the grandiose O'Connell memorial church in the centre of Cahersiveen had a

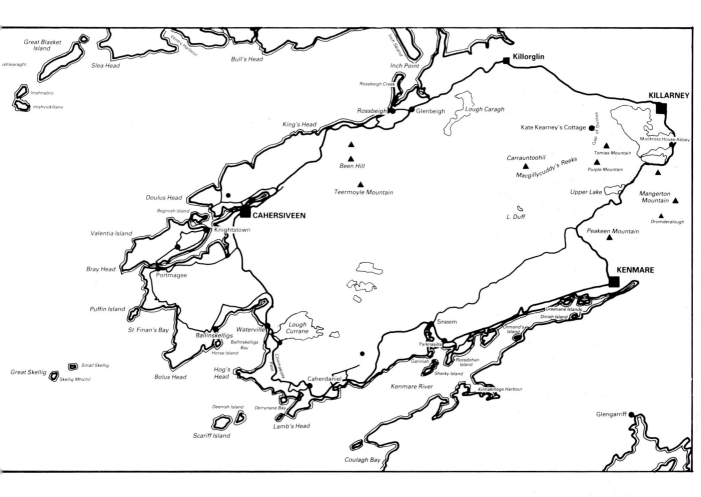

THE RING OF KERRY

Above: Rich contrasting colours in the mountain landscape near Killarney.

Left: Rossbeigh sands, one of the beautiful detours off the Ring of Kerry.

history befitting such a colourful advocate. Canon Brosnan, parish priest at Cahersiveen in 1875, planned to erect a memorial church to commemorate the centenary of O'Connell's birth, but both the bishop of Kerry and the archbishop of Cashel refused permission on the grounds that the George Ashlin plans were too elaborate. Undaunted, Canon Brosnan went direct to Rome where Pope Leo XIII not only gave his blessing to the project but even sent a stone from the Catacombs to be the corner stone and ordered Archbishop Croke of Cashel to lay it in 1888! This was done, and the church, although missing the centenary by quite a few years, was built. However, financial strictures prevented the completion of the planned spire. Perhaps if the church had been constructed economically of local sandstone rather than Newry granite the spire could also now dominate Cahersiveen's skyline.

Another building of note in Cahersiveen is the ruin of a magnificent police barracks of a peculiarly ornate design. The local explanation for this unreal Kerry building is that the plans for a Cahersiveen barracks became mixed up with plans for a barracks designed for the north-west frontier of India. In any case, the building was burned in the War of Independence 1919-22, but its strange stone structure still serves to puzzle the inquiring observer.

Two miles (3km) north of Cahersiveen, on another worthwhile detour, stands another building of O'Connell connection - the remains of the magnificent fifteenth-century McCarthy More castle at Ballycarbery, where O'Connell's ancestors were guardians until transported to Clare by the Cromwellian settlements of the seventeenth century. And conveniently nearby, standing conspicuously on a rock outcrop, is a national monument from another period - the stone-built and well-repaired fort of Leacanabuaile. Excavations here in 1939-40 yielded iron knives and pins, bone and combs, whetstones and millstones - rather meagre in quantity but enough to date the fort and its enclosed buildings to the ninth or tenth century A.D.

VALENTIA ISLAND

Following the Ring again westward from Cahersiveen the principal features of Valentia Island, including the conspicuous white-painted waterfront terraces of the former Transatlantic Telegraph Station (now private residences), are so clearly visible from the main Ring road that the island readily invites a detour and a visit in its own right.

Knightstown, the island's capital village, is named after the former local landlord, the Knight of Kerry, who, in his time, surrounded his home at Glanleam on the northern shore of Valentia with a famous private garden of trees and rare shrubs. The disused slate quarry in the island's Geokaun mountain high above Knightstown has been converted into an impressive religious grotto, and the views of Dingle Bay and Valentia Harbour from this vantage point are quite exceptionally beautiful. In Valentia Harbour the tiny Church Island - not to be confused with Church Island at Waterville - boasts an Early Christian settlement, and Beginish Island - not to be confused with Beginish in the Blasket group - was the site of a Viking settlement in the ninth-tenth centuries. But the harbour's main feature was always its deep water and good shelter. Little wonder that the Cromwellians in the 1640s-50s erected two forts to guard it, one of which is now Valentia lighthouse.

From Valentia's pre-history comes the druid figure Mogh Ruith, 'Servant of the Wheel', chief druid of Ireland - a sun-god symbol with a white, flaming, sky-flying chariot, and such formidable powers that the King of Cashel frequently sent gifts of cattle to keep this character pacified! (*See also Island's section for more information on Valentia*).

The main Ring highway to Waterville offers little in comparison to the many interesting little minor routes running in the same direction towards Waterville. As many detours as possible are advised!

FINAN'S BAY

Killabuonia overlooking Finan's Bay, is an Early Christian settlement which occupies the site of an earlier pagan centre. The Gallarus-type oratories and beehive huts are in a ruined state but the site gives the best mainland impression of the Skellig

Mhichíl island settlement which by comparison is so well preserved.

The ruined romanesque church at Killemlagh, also overlooking Finan's Bay, marks the site of another sixth-century monastery founded by St Fionan, and the same hillside also offers relics of the Bronze Age – two well-preserved wedge graves and a gallan (standing stone). The beautiful sandy beach at Finan's Bay is a wonderful amenity, but cross-currents at the western extremity deserve some caution.

BALLINSKELLIGS BAY

Overlooking the miles of sandy beach at Ballinskelligs Bay is the ruin of another McCarthy castle, and nearby, struggling against sea erosion, are the Augustinian Priory remains, so closely associated with the Skellig Mhichíl monastic settlement, and to which — according to the Welsh diarist Giraldus Cambrensis — the Skellig community retired when they vacated the Skellig monastery around the twelfth century A.D.

Ballinskelligs is an Irish-speaking area. It is also an area of dwindling population, and on a detour off our current detour the cul-de-sac roadway to Bolus Head is both majestic in its scenery and poignant in its deserted Famine cottages.

WATERVILLE

Waterville and Ballinskelligs Bay feature in many legends. First was the arrival of Ceasair to escape the Flood. Noah excluded his son Bith and Bith's daughter, Ceasair, from the Ark. So she set sail for Ireland, which, her wizards said, being uninhabited, sinless and free of reptiles and monsters, would escape the flood. Eventually three ships reached here, but two were wrecked and their crews drowned. The third ship with Ceasair, her father, Bith, two other men and forty-nine women landed on Saturday 5th, or perhaps the 15th, of the month (but it is not clear what month) in the year 2958 B.C.! The three men divided the fifty women between them. The pilot, Ladra, died shortly afterwards. The women were re-apportioned between Bith and the third man, Fintan, Ceasair's choice; but Bith also died. This was too much for the remaining Fintan. He fled from them all, whereupon Ceasair died of a broken heart. Fintan, in various forms, including a period as a one-eyed salmon, survived to tell the story.

LOUGH CURRANE

Near Waterville is Lough Currane around which are many Early Christian remains – stone forts, beehive huts and old roadways, with, on Church Island, another settlement attributed to St Fionan and the ruins of a fine romanesque church. The lake is a great centre for salmon, sea trout and brown trout. It was formerly named after the god Lug, whose wife was said to be buried in the great dolmen at Waterville House.

EIGHTERCUA

The four stones at Eightercua, only a stone's throw from Lough Currane, are the reputed burial place of Scéne – wife of one of the eight leaders of the Milesians in the last and greatest of the legendary invasions of Ireland – who died at sea before the fleet landed near Waterville on Thursday, 1 May, 1700 B.C.! Beyond Waterville as the Ring road leaves Ballinskelligs Bay the two Skelligs rocks come into view, the small Skellig white with thousands of gannets – it is one of the great gannetries of the world – and the Great Skellig, or Skellig Mhichíl, which has on it in most perfect form a simple monastic settlement occupied between the sixth and twelfth centuries. (*See Islands section*).

COOMAKISTA PASS AND DERRYNANE

Coomakista Pass leads the main road on to a new vista – Kenmare Bay, bordered on the distant county Cork coast by the Bull, Cow and Calf rocks and Dursey Island, and punctuated in the Kerry foreground by the sister islands of Scariff and Deenish. There are also views of Derrynane, with memories of Daniel O'Connell whose home it was. There are many vivid Derrynane tales from the eighteenth century about the O'Connell ancestors' export and import business. The imports included the wine and spirit produce of France and Spain – and a keg of brandy would go a long

*Above: Soft light over a typical
inland Kerry landscape at
Kilgarvan, near Kenmare.*

*Right: The Kenmare-Killarney road
is studded with breathtaking views –
here, the Macgillycuddy Reeks.*

way towards pacifying a local customs official or two. But the customs men at the time were more active and keen to close off the O'Connell export activities – transport of Irish Catholic students to Europe for an education which was denied to them as Catholics at home. It was not easy to outwit the old Gaelic O'Connell family on their home ground. They were a tough, adventurous people.

Daniel O'Connell's uncle, Maurice, accumulated a large fortune through his shipping ventures. This he left to Daniel, thus enabling him to devote himself to laying the foundations of Irish democracy.

Coad Mountain, overlooking Derrynane and the nearby Caherdaniel village, is a link with much earlier sea traffic, for its mountainside copper mines high above the coast are believed to have been the real incentive for the early Celtic invasions of Ireland some four thousand years ago. Some of the standing stones in this area are monuments to that period and their alignment may have been a pointer from the harbour to the copper mines above.

STAIGUE FORT

Staigue Fort, on a 4km cul-de-sac near Castlecove village, is one of the best-preserved ancient Irish structures, dating either from the Iron Age of 500 B.C. or the Early Christian period. Stone forts are many in the area but none have such sophistication as Staigue nor such architecturally beautiful

Derrynane House, Co. Kerry

Above: An old photograph of the O'Connell home at Derrynane.

Right: Staigue Fort, a well-preserved, ancient defence structure.

features as Staigue's internal X shaped stone stairways. And Staigue had up-market inhabitants! This is indicated by the fact that the fort had interior buildings of wood, which have long since disappeared.

SNEEM

The colourful village of Sneem is renowned for its brightly painted façades, its frequent success in the Tidy Towns awards and for its growing collection of international monumental art. The third Earl of Dunraven, who formerly owned Garinish Island at the mouth of the Sneem river, was also the donor of the village's Italianate church which dates from 1865.

At Sneem the Ring of Kerry traveller has the option of taking the short cut to Killarney – a very beautiful short cut through wild, desolate terrain of mountain and bogland via Moll's Gap – or the second option of taking the fuller circuit to Kenmare via G.B. Shaw's hideaway at Parknasilla where he wrote much of his famous play, *St Joan*. This longer route eventually joins the Moll's Gap road leading back to Killarney.

The Castle of Dromore, subject of the well known lullaby, is hidden in Dromore Forest on the approach to Kenmare. This castle was the seat of an old Gaelic family, the O'Mahony's, one of whom, Captain Dan O'Mahony, gained international renown for leading the famous Irish defence against the surprise attack on Cremona in Lombardy in 1703. The town, as anyone might guess from the proponderance of the O'Sullivan name, was the ancient seat of that great Gaelic clan which occupied both sides of Kenmare Bay from the twelfth century until they were ousted by the Cromwellians in the seventeenth century and the lands fell into the ownership of the ubiquitous Petty, who was the founder of the town in 1670. Petty's descendant, the first Marquis of Lansdowne, laid out the basic plan of the present town in 1775. Nearby Dunkerron Castle and the very ruined earlier remains on its grounds constitute today's mementos of the great O'Sullivan Mór.

As a valuable incentive to complete the Ring, nature has strewn the main road from Kenmare to Killarney with the most magnificent views of mountain and lake scenery; and man has helped, for much of this area now falls within the new and expanding boundaries of Muckross National Park and is thus safeguarded for ever.

Muckross House, Killarney, full of fascinating history and in a most beautiful setting, now a National Park.

MUCKROSS HOUSE

Killarney's Muckross House, now run by the state as a museum, is the final gem on the Ring. Administrative and cultural centre of the National Park, it specialises in the artefacts and traditions of Kerry. And not just the old and the obsolete find a home here; this is a vibrant place where culture and custom actually live – in crafts, in exhibitions, in farming methods. The taste of its architect, the style of the former owners (the Herberts) and the enthusiasm of the present management all shine through. Here in a splendid setting of natural and manmade garden is a truly magnificent house, built of Portland stone, which was quarried in England, shipped to Kenmare and carted across the mountains in 1843 to a site which prompted the celebrated Bishop Berkeley to exclaim, 'Another Louis XIV may make another Versailles, but the hand of the Deity only can make another Muckross.'

The Dingle Peninsula

Above: Smerwick Harbour taken from Ballydavid Head. The Blaskets are
in the distance – from the right, Inishtooskert, Inishtearacht, Inishnabro,
Great Blasket.
Right: Near the Conor Pass – the Pass is 416 metres high and provides
panoramic views to the north and to the south of the Dingle Peninsula.

The Dingle Peninsula

This peninsula is one of the most beautiful and rugged places in Ireland. It is the most westerly part of the country and includes, literally, the 'next parish to America'. There is exceptional variety and richness in the prehistoric and Early Christian remains. Two thousand sites have been identified and some thirty-eight of Kerry's national monuments are located in this 50km by 20km limb of land. Tour guides suggest that the peninsula may be covered in a day, but what a superficial dash that would be! The Dingle Peninsula must be taken at leisure, for it is a journey into the archaeological past.

The Slieve Mish mountains, rising steeply over Castlemaine Harbour and forming the backbone of the peninsula, give a good preview of the terrain – steep climbs, zigzag roads and a multiplicity of ancient sites, some of which are mythical such as Scotia's Grave — burial place of Scotia, widow of the invader Milesius who was killed in battle with the goddess Dana; and some very real and impressive such as the ancient, almost inaccessible Iron Age inland promontory fort near the summit of Caherconree Mountain, 2715ft (1264m) above the sea. But even this place had its mystical characters: the fort was the reputed home of a legendary

hero or god, Curoi mac Dara, and the legend recalls a clash between Curoi and Cuchulainn over a woman, Blathnaid, and how Curoi humiliated Cuchulainn and carried the girl to the mountain. Cuchulainn, seeking revenge, and still seeking the girl, came to the bottom of the mountain and met Blathnaid. She arranged to get Curoi to disperse the garrison, and gave the signal to Cuchulainn to attack the fort. Cuchulainn attacked, killed Curoi, and carried Blathnaid off. Curoi's druid, Fercheirtne, who had helplessly watched the murder of his master, went with them. One day, when they were on a high cliff overlooking the sea, he suddenly seized Blathnaid and jumped over the cliff so that they were both dashed to death below.

Not everyone will opt for such an adventurous climb as Caherconree on the first touring day. Indeed, the beautiful Inch Strand at the southern lead-in to the peninsula may be so inviting as to terminate any further travels – even for the history hunter, for here, as well as miles of silver beach are the sandhill sites which yielded the shell middens that vaguely suggest habitation of seven thousand years ago!

Shaking off the lethargy of a beautiful day on a beautiful beach and moving gently westward along the peninsula in search of further fact or fiction, the inquiring visitor is drawn to Anascaul, scene of another Cuchulainn legend (Lake Anascaul is well distanced from any main road, but its striking, boulder-strewn terrain has to be

seen to get the full impact of the story): A giant tried to take away a local girl, Scál ní Mhurnain, but Cuchulainn sprang to the rescue. From the mountains on each side of the lake, Cuchulainn and the giant hurled great boulders at each other, littering the slopes with their battle debris. Cuchulainn was hit and wounded, and Scál, thinking him dead, threw herself into the lake. It has borne her name ever since, and the great missiles of Cuchulainn and the giant still cover the surrounding slopes!

An inquiring student of botany and medicine may well want to make a detour from this lake to the nearby pass of Gleann na Gealt – Madmen's Glen – to check out its chemistry, for the story goes that this valley was so named not for causing the said mental affliction, but for curing it through drinking the local water and consuming the local herbs.

Diversions on the route from Anascaul to Dingle are many; the great gallan of Ballineetig at Lispole, the largest Bronze Age gravestone on the peninsula, is awe-inspiring; the marble-sized pebbles perfectly graded by nature on Kinard Beach are another cause for wonder; even, on the outskirts of Dingle, the detour to Emlagh East is hard to omit, for here, now lying horizontally, is the Priest's Stone. This is the ogham stone first noticed by the Welsh antiquarian Edward Lluyd in the eighteenth century, then moved to Tralee by Lord Ventry in the mid-nineteenth century, and subsequently returned to its present position because of

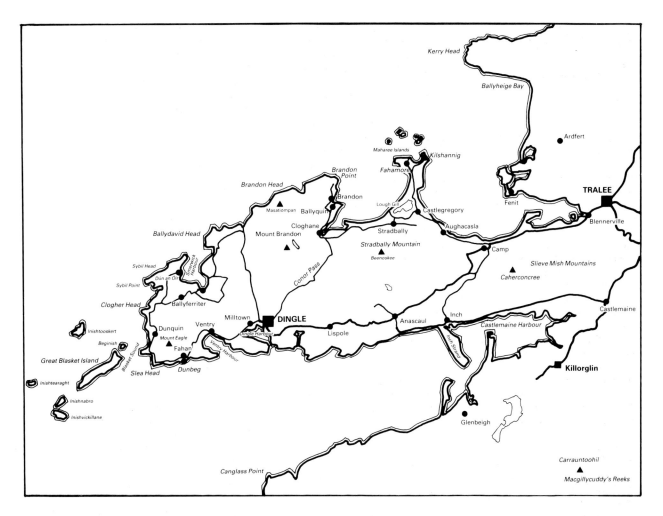

THE DINGLE PENINSULA

Dingle Harbour, a lively fishing port.

threats by nationalists against the absentee landlords. Ballintaggart (the Priest's Village) on the same byroad will likewise be engrossing for in this burial ground there are nine ogham stones, some with writing and some with crosses, suggesting a transitional phase from paganism to Christianity.

DINGLE

Dingle is a lively and colourful town once heavily dependent on fishing but now also much involved in tourism since the 1970 film *Ryan's Daughter* displayed the peninsula's scenery to the world. In medieval times Dingle was the principal harbour in Kerry, having an extensive wine trade and a degree of intimacy with France that might well have altered somewhat the course of Europe's history had Marie Antoinette accepted the invitation of Kerry's Count Rice to take refuge in 'the highest house in Dingle' at the time of the French Revolution!

Of modern services, Dingle has good restaurants and an excellent bookshop, but for all its four-hundred-year-old history the town has little that is ancient. The exceptions are the 'holy stone', an enormous pock-marked rock at the side of Main Street, which may have been a means of grinding grain in Early Christian times; and the Pictorial Stones, one of which bears the date 1586, now set into the plastered façades of Green Street's modern houses.

Across the harbour from Dingle town is a girls' school, Coláiste Íde, formerly the home of the Lords Ventry, one of whom in the pre-Famine years 1820-40 was a major supporter of the strong Protestant missionary effort in the area. But travelling westwards from the town one quickly leaves these relatively modern times behind. The Gates of Glory, two standing stones near Milltown Bridge, reach far back into the past and mysterious rock scribblings there may well have been the work of those metal prospectors who came to Kerry from Europe about four thousand years ago.

Ventry Harbour, beach-lined, sheltered and inviting today, was once the scene of a great legendary battle: Fionn Mac Cumhail eloped (yet again!) with both the wife and daughter of the King of France. The King, with the aid of the King of Spain and the King of the World arrived at Ventry, filling the bay with their ships. The Fianna, Fionn's army of warriors, managed to keep them at bay for a year and a day. The King of Spain was killed in the fighting and the King of France went mad! However, the invaders had with them a giant who managed each day to slay his opponent. Finally, a group of boys arrived from Ulster to challenge the giant, and all were killed but for one, the king of Ulster's own son, who clung to the giant so fiercely that they both drowned in the incoming tide.

Ventry is another moment of truth for the tour guide. Is it to be the coastal road onwards to Slea Head taking in the fine

A colourful shopfront in Dingle town.

promontory fort on the cliffs at Dunbeg and the hillside village of ancient beehive dwellings, cave dwellings, standing and inscribed stones, stone crosses, souterrains, forts, cahers and a church at Fahan? Or will it be the inland route from Ventry to Dunquin across the old Mám Clasach mountain pass to savour in one sudden visual shock-wave the immense and beautiful panorama of the whole Blasket Island group that springs into view from the summit of the pass? Or perhaps it will be the Ventry-Ballyferriter route, seeing Rahinnane Castle and spending hours admiring and dreaming about the mysterious and exquisite La Tène (European Celtic) art on the famous inscribed cross at Reasc? Indeed, perhaps the day will be spent neither among castles nor clochans, standing stones nor souterrains, beaches nor breathtaking scenery, but listening to, enjoying and hopefully joining in with the beautiful spoken native Irish language still so vibrantly alive in this part of the west.

Dunbeg, a promontory fort clinging to the cliffs.

SLEA HEAD

Nowhere in Kerry does the main road make more close contact with the open Atlantic than at Slea Head and from this high vantage point the Blasket Islands, the Iveragh Peninsula, distant Skellig rocks, the whole expanse of Dingle Bay and the open Atlantic ocean can be appreciated and put into context. Indeed, the rather frightening view of the wrecked cargo ship *Ranga* on the nearby rocks of Dunmore Head is a grim reminder that the enticing blue ocean of a fine summer's day is seldom in the same sweet humour on a winter's night. The retreating remnants of the Spanish Armada also found this out to their cost in September 1588, when two ships, their sails in tatters, were driven to their doom in the same waters of the Blasket Sound. Even the beautiful Coumeenole Beach at the foot of Slea Head needs to be treated with a little caution due to currents at the western (right hand) extremity.

DUNQUIN

Dunquin is the gateway to those so near yet so far Blasket Islands which in their time have produced several important literary works in Irish. Even the dramatic flight of steps set into the rock face leading down to Dunquin harbour is already an adventure!

This is the home of the typical local canvas-covered canoe, the *naomhóg*. These boats are built of long timber laths, curved high at the bow to ride the Atlantic swell, the shape and lightness of this vessel making it extraordinarily seaworthy in experienced hands. The black tarred canvas shape makes a striking sight when floating lightly on the sea but even more so at launch time when the six legs of the fishermen walk the upturned beatle-like boat down to the water's edge.

From Dunquin northwards towards Ballyferriter the coast-hugging main road leads inevitably to Clogher Strand, another of the peninsula's beauty spots. Here the adventuresome and the curious will want to abandon the highway and venture into the byways of Ferriter's Cove and the pathways of Sybil Point, Smerwick ('butter harbour' from the Viking name) and Dún an Óir.

The ruined Castle Sybil of the Anglo-Norman Ferriters was built inside an Iron Age promontory fort and was named after Sybil Lynch of Galway who eloped with a Ferriter and who was drowned by the rising tide in a nearby cave whilst hiding from her irate father.

Also nearby, inside another Iron Age fort, lies the sixteenth-century Dún an Óir, the 'Fort of Gold'. But the Fort of Gold, however, has no romantic anecdote to dilute its gruesome past, for Dún an Óir experienced the harshest massacre in a period of harsh massacres. An expedition of six hundred people, mostly Italians but also including Spanish, English and Irish, were financed by the Pope to go to Ireland to support the cause of the Catholic Irish against the Protestant English. They arrived here at Dún an Óir in September 1580, and were the first significant assistance to come into Ireland for many centuries. But the promontory fort where they set up defences was easily surrounded. The English soldiers under Lord Grey bombarded Dún and Óir from the land and Admiral Winter's fleet laid siege to it from the sea. Soon, the fort's defenders surrendered. However, once disarmed they were slaughtered – men, women and children. This massacre was broadcast throughout Europe as a warning against sending further assistance to the Irish. Sir Walter Raleigh was probably present at the event as was Edmund Spenser.

BALLYFERRITER

Ballyferriter's small village and its sparsely populated surrounding

Dunquin Harbour, the departure point for the trip to the Great Blasket and the home of the naomhóg, the traditional lightweight, skin-covered boat.

A dramatic view of Rahinnane Castle, on the Ventry-Ballyferriter route.

lowland may have every appearance of being a sleepy backwater, but what a false impression that is! This place is the power-house of the peninsula's cooperative development society, Comharchumann Forbartha Chorca Dhuibhne, which among other activities has furthered the investigation of many of the surrounding archaeological sites, furthered the growth of Irish-language summer schools, and greatly advanced the peninsula's economic development. Fishing is one of the conspicuous summertime activities and Smerwick Harbour's small landing place at Ballydavid can scarcely cater for the influx of boats from all over Kerry and, indeed, from parts of the west Cork coast as well, over the summer months.

GALLARUS

On land this influx is matched, and well exceeded, by the many visitors who come from all over the world to view the priceless local archaeological gem, the boat-shaped Gallarus Oratory. This is the most perfect piece of early Irish building. It is the best example of dry rubble masonry in Ireland, or indeed in the world. Such oratories were standard on monastic sites, but everywhere except here and on the Skelligs the unmortared roofs have fallen in from the weight of the stones. Gallarus probably dates from the eighth century.

BRANDON CREEK

St Brendan's sixth-century voyages, possibly even to America, set off from this peninsula, and the tiny, rock-bound creek on the northernmost tip of the headland was his departure point. Not everyone may wish to follow Brendan's voyages out to sea but quite near here is the Saints' Road, which allows one to follow his footsteps to the site of his mountaintop hermitage on the 953 metre-high Mount Brandon. This was a common penitential pilgrimage in medieval times, and the account of Brendan's life, written in Latin in the ninth century, became immensely popular in medieval Europe. The Mount Brandon

Kilmalkedar Church near Gallarus Oratory, one of the finest romanesque churches in the country, with an ogham stone in the foreground.

pilgrimage route is occasionally followed nowadays, but only when weather conditions are very safe and suitable.

A road on the seaward side of Mount Brandon would make an interesting, scenic and convenient short circuit from Brandon Creek to Brandon Point and Cloghane, but no such road exists, nor is planned! Meanwhile, the obligatory return to Dingle to gain access to the Conor Pass is hardly an undue hardship to the modern traveller and the view from the top of this pass, 416m high, taking in Dingle Bay to the south and Tralee Bay, Brandon Bay and even the far-off mouth of the Shannon to the north, will be ample reward.

CLOGHANE

Cloghane was, up to recent times, the site of the traditional end-of-July festival celebrating the triumph of the pagan god Lug over another pagan deity. Since Christian times such celebrations gained respectability through the suggestion that the festival actually celebrated the conversion of the local magician, Crom Dubh, to Christianity. In the chancel wall of the ruined Protestant church is a carved head believed to be that of Crom Dubh, possibly the only pagan head surviving in this part of Ireland. To kiss this head was traditionally regarded as a cure for chronic toothache!

The other local pagan legend tells the story of the voyage of the mythical warrior Bran and his companions to the magical western islands, where they spent

what they thought was a year on the Island of Women. On their return voyage, however, when one of the crew, Nechtan, jumped ashore at Brandon Point, he immediately turned into ashes, thus indicating that they had been away for a very long time indeed. Bran and his companions quickly turned back to the western ocean, and were never heard of again. This, according to one story, is how Brandon got its name.

Beautiful beaches follow mile upon mile as the coastal road now leads back out of the peninsula — Brandon, Cloghane, Stradbally . . . And in the lowland dunes of Castlegregory is the added attraction of Lough Gill, wintertime haunt of many wildbirds, including the Bewick's swan.

For anyone who has not yet had their fill of antiquity, Kilshannig offers an enormous gallan, a ruined parish church and a seventh-century crosspillar. And the island of Illauntannig, just off the Maharee Peninsula, has yet another ruined Christian monastery. At Castlegregory the weary traveller is only fifteen miles from Tralee. The circuit has been completed, but vows will be made to return again very soon.

Ancient field patterns at Fahan, near Slea Head.

Mount Brandon in the early morning.

Islands

The Kerry islands, standing so disdainfully off the coast, cajole many visitors to brave the waves and tauntingly dare the viewer: Visit me — if you can. Perhaps it is for this challenge, perhaps it is for the sheer grandeur of their solitary independence that man over the centuries has endured so many hardships to visit the islands, to settle there and to live and die there. The well-known archaeological remains on many Kerry islands are conclusive proof of habitation back to the Early Christian era, and, in Valentia, for example, now coming to light are other indications of much earlier civilisations, so that one visit, one holiday week, one lifetime, would not be enough to know the islands intimately! Indeed, occasional, would-be island-visitors have often sat out their entire holiday marooned on the mainland, scarcely able to catch a glimpse of their inaccessible, befogged destination across raging, relentless seas.

Fortunately, such conditions do not always prevail, and the more important islands are generally accessible in the summer months. But this is not to say that a full-scale passenger service exists. Local fishing boats fill the bill in most cases and consequently it is only through local inquiry that you can feel your way out to the islands.

At least nobody needs a boat to get to Derrynane's Abbey Island. You can walk along a neck of sand to this interesting place at all but the highest tide. Here are the ruins of Aghavore Abbey, dating from the ninth or tenth century, and reputedly standing on the monastic site founded by St Fionan Cam – as distinct from Fionan the Leper – some centuries earlier. Here, too, is the burial place of Tomás Rua O'Súilleabháin, (1785-1848), schoolmaster, story-teller, fiddler, and poet in the Irish language. Within walking distance in the surrounding region are other interesting options: Derrynane House, home of O'Súilleabháin's better-known contemporary, also patron and friend, Daniel O'Connell (1775-1847), is now a museum to O'Connell's life and times.

Nearby is the Derrynane ogham stone, interpreted to read: 'The name of Llatign, son of Minerc, descendant of Q....c'. And embracing all these components is Derrynane's magnificent beach and the Derrynane Dunes Nature Trail – the first seaside nature trail in the Republic of Ireland, which carefully outlines the developing, but fragile, dune ecology. (*See Ring of Kerry section.*)

Out at sea, 5 miles (8km) south-west of Derrynane, and easily visible from the coast, Scariff Island – 260 metres in height – and its little sister, Deenish, 146 metres, sit together and wait! They have seen much smuggling history sail by in the activities of Daniel O'Connell's ancestors. They have seen the Cromwellian brutality of 1653 when Friar Francis O'Sullivan of Tuosist, Provincial of the Franciscan House in Ireland, was captured and beheaded on Scariff. And an even older gruesome tale survives from the end of the fourteenth century, when an English expeditionary vessel commanded by Sir John Arundel ran into storm difficulties at Scariff - the ship was crewed by an unruly mob, which, having snatched a number of nuns from a convent in Cornwall en route, and having subjected them to 'scenes of frightful debauchery' on board, later flung the women ruthlessly overboard in an effort to lighten the load on the sinking ship!

Today the only visible signs of the past on Scariff are some small building remains which may include a Bronze Age settlement and a Christian anchorite site.

Wandering westwards along the many minor roads which hug the shoreline of this Kerry barony of Iveragh, the island-hunter is rewarded with breathtaking glimpses of such gems as Puffin Island, Small Skellig and Skellig Mhichíl, reaching out like a chain of giant stepping-stones to the Atlantic horizon south-west of Valentia. Here indeed are island centres of ornithology and archaeology which are world famous, their importance far exceeding anything that their size or obscure location would suggest.

Puffin Island, covering an area of 122 acres (51 hectares), and rising some 170 metres above the sea, is the nearest of the trio, being separated from the coast by a channel of some 400 metres in width. But what a wild, stormy and impassable channel this can be! The island has not been inhabited in recent history, and the remains of small field boundaries and of a beehive hut near the landing place of the north-eastern end of the island may have been an Early Christian settlement. But Puffin Island's real fame is as a wildbird sanctuary, owned and administered by the Irish Wildbird Conservancy. As such, it is home to 20,000 pairs of Manx shearwater (*Puffinus puffinus*), one of the largest colonies of this species in north-west Europe. It is also home to 10,000 pairs of puffin (*Fratercula arctica*), 1,000 pairs of storm petrel (*Hydrobates pelagicus*) and 600 pairs of fulmar (*Fulmarus glacialis*), as well as many of the other, more common, seabirds. This island has no real landing facility, except the option of scrambling from boat to rock-face, and consequently is seldom visited except by ornithological work-parties in temporary summer camps.

Five miles farther out to sea, the gaunt and craggy Small Skellig, also administered by the Conservancy as a sanctuary, is a strange contrast. It has no shearwater and no puffin, but every conceivable ledge of its 16 acres (6.5 hectares), right to the 135-metre summit, is covered with 23,000 pairs of goose-sized gannets (*Sula bassana*) – one of the largest colonies in the world! In its deep surrounding waters you may sail to within a few metres of Small Skellig's sheer cliffs; you may sail around it or sail through the centre of it – as Small Skellig is really two rocks rather than one – but landing on this place is out of the question!

Landing on the nearby Skellig Mhichíl, the final link in the island chain, is relatively easy at the small pier which was built by the lighthouse authorities in 1826, and this 44-acre (18-hectare), 220-metre-high island provides a further contrast in wildlife: it has no gannets but has all the other seabirds in thousands and tens of thousands, nesting within an arm's reach of the lighthouse roadway.

But outweighing these riches of nature, Skellig Mhichíl's feast of archaeological remains, in the shape of a well-preserved, sixth-century monastic settlement perched on a ledge 184 metres above the sea, is Kerry's – and Ireland's – most spectacular, most impressive, most memorable national monument. Words cannot adequately describe the little village of beehive-shaped huts and oratories where a monastic community lived and worked and prayed from the sixth century to the twelfth century. Skelling must be seen to be believed.

Closer to the Kerry coast, and linked to the mainland by bridge since 1970, Valentia Island is slowly yielding secrets of a much older habitation, a habitation of some three thousand years ago. In the island's cut-away bogs, old fences and old cooking places are coming to light, and pollen analysis techniques on this period are showing evidence of intensive husbandry ultimately falling into

The well-preserved, sixth-century monastery on Skellig Mhichíl. In the distance is Small Skellig, home to 23,000 pairs of gannets.

53

Above: Derrynane Harbour (where the O'Connell ancestors carried out their smuggling activities) – here you can walk to Abbey Island with its ruins of Aghavore Abbey.
Left: The Blasket Islands, the most westerly part of Ireland.

slow decline, and evidence of substantial oak forests giving way to cultivation and subsequently to nettles and weeds and peat growth. It is a study which has only recently begun and no doubt will yield many more answers as time goes on.

But in more modern times Valentia is better known in other ways. This island was the European terminus of the first transatlantic telegraph cable in 1855, and for a century was a vital link in world communications until the closure of that system in 1966. Also, Valentia radio station is another pioneer, and has since 1912 provided sterling communications service to seafarers of all nations. Valentia weather observatory is a well-known reference for many people, but of course this establishment, founded on the island in 1876 and with delightful ambiguity retaining that name, has been in Cahersiveen since 1892!

Valentia, with a population of some 700, and an area of 6,368 acres (2,653 hectares) is one of Ireland's largest islands. Its name is generally kept in the public eye today as home port of Valentia lifeboat which frequently makes national headlines whenever misfortunate seafarers and the Atlantic ocean are at loggerheads anywhere between Bantry Bay and the Shannon Estuary.

Beginish Island, small and sandy-beached, in the northern part of Valentia Harbour is scarcely significant one would think. Yet, it has produced a significant artefact from the past – a stone which bore rare inscriptions of Viking origin: 'Lir erected this stone; M... carved the runes'. A full report of this excavation is published by O'Kelly (1956) and the stone now rests in University College, Cork.

Nearby Church Island, though scarcely 100 metres in diameter, has the remains of a small monastic settlement which may date from A.D. 750, but this has suffered considerably in modern times from the ravages of weather and the burrowing of rabbits. It is nonetheless a national monument.

On the northern shores of Dingle Bay the Blasket Islands, consisting of six islands and hundreds of dangerous rocks, are the weatherbeaten outriders of the Dingle Peninsula. Inishtearaght, with a lighthouse, and currently a three-man crew, is the most westerly inhabited part of Europe, some nine miles from the Slea Head mainland, from which the most magnificent island views can be seen. Next, in terms of 'westerness', comes Inishvickillane, then Inishnabro, Inishtooskert, Great Blasket and Beginish. Though big and bold and dominating every sea view from the mainland, the outer islands are well isolated by nature and are seldom visited casually.

Great Blasket, some 6km by 1km in extent, is the exception. Its tiny landing place sees many, many visitors throughout the summer – film-makers, writers, students, historians, artists, wanderers, families – driven here by the urge to experience in daydreams the wild and beautiful and cruel life so poignantly depicted in the renowned books which have emanated from this place.

Anyone who has read *Twenty Years A-Growing* by Maurice O'Sullivan must pilgrimage here and imagine themselves scampering along in the innocent company of young Maurice and Tomas Owen Vaun as they risked their lives daily on the island's cliffs to hunt puffins and rabbits:

The ruined village on Great Blasket, once the home of a small but highly developed community.

'A cold sweat was coming out on me with the eeriness of the place. I stopped and looked up. When I saw the black rugged cliff standing straight above me I began to tremble still more. I looked down and there was nothing below me but the blue depth of the sea: 'God of Virtues!' I cried, 'isn't it a dangerous place I am in!'

To read Tomás O'Crohan's *The Islandman* will draw the Blasket visitor down to the island's beautiful White Strand, to stand alone there and think the sombre thoughts of the ageing Tomás as he retells his memories:

'The boats took up the other two just as Pats and I were returning as usual from fishing. That was the sight that awaited us ... The 'other two' were the bodies of Eileen Nicholls from Dublin and O'Crohan's son, who had vainly tried to save her from drowning.'

And those who have read *An Old Woman's Reflections* by Peig Sayers – the mainland girl who married into the Blasket community – will have to follow her footsteps here, sit on the island's slopes, and gaze down across Peig's now-deserted, ruined village – a place which once knew, and handled equally philosophically, hardship and heartache, emigration and earthen-floor dancing, song and sudden death. And then awake with a jolt from the reverie, to wonder why someone does not keep a door and a roof and a window in these monuments so that another generation might appreciate that the now nettle-grown hearths of Sayers, O'Crohan and O'Sullivan are as important a factor in the heritage of Corca Dhuibhne as Gallarus Oratory or the inscribed cross slab of Reasc!

The final, but by no means least important, of Kerry's ocean islands are the Seven Hogs or Maharee Islands off the Castlegregory Peninsula. Illauntannig, largest and most accessible of the group, has significant Early Christian buildings attributed to St Senan (or Senach) and, although the inroads of the sea into the soft limestone here and the wear and tear of time have not been kind, the remains of a heavy cashel wall, two oratories, three beehive huts and some burial places still survive. Inishtooskert, the most remote island of the Maharees, has featured in another period of Irish history. For it was here that the ill-fated gun-running ship, the *Aud*, under Captain Spindler, with a cargo of arms from Germany to aid the planned Irish rebellion in 1916, arrived on the night of Holy Thursday. The local sea-pilot who was to take the ship to a safe landing place failed to keep the rendezvous because of a confusion about the date of arrival of the ship. This delay – and efficient spying – led to the capture of the *Aud* by the British, and the dashing of Irish hopes for foreign help.

An allied disaster for the Irish rebels occurred on the same weekend on nearby Banna Strand. Roger Casement, who had been in Germany on a separate mission – trying to get support from Irish members of the British Army for the proposed rising – also arrived in a German submarine in the Tralee Bay area. He landed in a dinghy at Banna Strand and was captured and subsequently executed.

Flora

'Hurry and noise are the keynotes of today, and where these prevail we need never hope to lure the fairies from their hiding places.' These are the words of Robert Lloyd Praeger, 1856-1953. And if there is still a time and a place for random, unguided wandering, the place is Kerry, and the time is now.

And 'now' does not have to be the midsummer months of July or August. April is full of colour; that lowly furze bush (*Ulex europaeus*), so readily dismissed by everyone as a blight upon the land, will provide a frame of brilliant yellow for every scene. May is the time for rhododendrons (*Rhododendron ponticum*), and on the shores of Caragh Lake every branch will dance in red and mauve, and a dozen hues in between. Walk in June on a soft pink carpet of thrift (*Armeria maritima*) on every sea-cliff. September hills, both near and far, will still be purple with the billion 'Chinese lantern' bells of heather (*Erica*), and on a fine midwinter's day the low-angled sun will add new shapes, dimensions and silhouettes to the mountain backdrop of every Kerry view, as well as adding a further range of colours – the tortured brown of bogland, the forty shades of cloud-grey, and the white, white rim on every sea-coast.

Of the colourful, hedgerow shrubs, fuchsia (*Fuchsia magellacina*) and Kerry are synonymous. These familiar red and mauve bells were an imported novelty just over a century ago, but now have run riot in the mild, equitable climate, and provide a blaze of colour throughout the county from May onwards.

RARE PLANTS

But the exciting plants of Kerry do not have to be great in stature, brilliant in colour or rich in perfume. On the banks of the muddy Cashen river the discovery of the dwarf spike-rush (*Scirpus nanus*), 25mm in height, and equally mundane in appearance, was enough to brighten a rather dull day for naturalist Robert L. Praeger. 'It is so rare that it is almost worth pilgrimaging to that dreary tract to gloat on its very insignificance'!

And there is still room for search and research in Kerry by both amateur and professional. Over three quarters of Ireland's 912 species of vascular plants are to be found in the county, and one quarter of all Ireland's rare plants are reputedly located there!

In all, fifty-two species of plants are protected under the 1976 Wildlife Act. If they are protected, then they are rare; and if they are rare, they are probably in Kerry, and are worth seeing, photographing or painting.

You can make some new, exotic friends perhaps no farther away than the nearest damp bank of Kerry's 129,000 acres (53,371 hectares) of bogland. This is the habitat of the greater butterwort (*Pinguicula grandiflora*), that violet-

The ubiquitous fuchsia, providing a colourful roadside hedgerow all over Kerry.

Right: Lakeside reeds at Muckross, Killarney.

flowered, yellow-leaved, insect-eating, Lusitanian beauty. The *Flora of County Kerry* (Scully, 1916) describes the butterwort in the most glowing terms: 'No one who has seen its groups of deep violet flowers – sometimes over an inch in diameter – on the black dripping rocks of Conor Hill, or on the boggy roadsides between Killarney and Kenmare, will deny its claim to be considered the most beautiful member of the Irish flora.'

An equally beautiful, but very rare, member of the Irish flora found only in Kerry is the Kerry lily (*Simethis planifolia*). The precise location of this slender, graceful, white-petalled, yellow-stamened, short-lived, mid-June wonder has been a well-kept secret, and, since it is high on the protected species list, nobody has dared to be more specific about its habitat than 'a few square miles of rocky heath in Kerry'. But be careful which rocky heath you tread in your search! The Kerry lily is only 25cm tall; its dark green leaves are almost grass-like, and its tiny flowers might easily be brushed aside or trampled – unseen, unrecognised – underfoot.

An even greater cloak of secrecy surrounds the location of another protected Kerry rarity, the Killarney fern (*Trichomanes speciosum*), and anyone who really knows where it exists in the wild is just not telling! But consider the clues: 1 There is a good dried example of the fern on display in Muckross House, Killarney; 2 In *An Irish Flora*, by D. A. Webb, there is an enlightening description of this reclusive, fragile, almost

transparent fern and of its typical habitat.

So, outdoor sleuth, with perseverance and sharp eyes and some adventure, you can perhaps find your own *Trichomanes speciosum*. It will be a thousand times more precious that way. But touch it not, and keep your secret for ever.

There are other less elusive, but no less wonderful, treasures to be noted along the Kerry wildflower trail. The strawberry tree (*Arbutus unedo*), a shrub of the Mediterranean, with edible if bitter fruits, widely displays its charming, cream-coloured, heather-like flowers around the Killarney woodland in September and October. And all over Kerry, on roadside, woodside and river bank, you will find the summer-long, two-tone green richness of Irish spurge (*Euphorbia hyberna*). St Patrick's cabbage (*Saxifraga spathularis*) is also abundant, its delicate pink flowers lighting up the undergrowth of old, damp woodlands or wet, rocky habitats from May to July. Its smaller relation, the white-flowered kidney-leaved saxifrage (*Saxifraga hirsuta*), is allegedly more rare, but the reverse is the case in the dim, damp Glanleam woods on Valentia Island.

Kerry is one of the few places too in Ireland to find the seaside pansy (*Viola curtisii*) – in sand dunes rather than rocky habitat. Pansy is a rather misleading name; the yellow or purple flowers resemble the pansy only in colour and shape, but in size the seaside pansy, by comparison, is minute.

WOODLAND

The Kerry nature garden is a big, varied garden, involving the most far-flung habitats: bog, river, lake, mudflat, ocean, rock, island and woodland. Of these, the woodland territory is the least known, and some of it is very new indeed. The Forest and Wildlife Service is conscious of the need to redress the many wrongs wreaked through the centuries upon the woodland structure of the county. Not only the sins of man are to blame, but also the perversity of nature, which, in the shape of ever-advancing bogland, was smothering prime forests long before man ever put his stone axe to the wood. Today in Kerry, in hundreds of woodland developments, new forests of pine (*Pinus*) and spruce (*Picea*) are covering some 39,000 acres (15,835 hectares).

Some purists would say that these dense conifers, which exclude so much light, are a hindrance rather than a help to other flora and fauna and that broadleaf native trees such as oak (*Quercus*), ash (*Fraxinus*) or beech (*Fagus*), would be more beneficial and more appropriate. But the economic considerations are equally valid. The conifers, although they are the offspring of relatively recent imports, are readily amenable to the poor soil of Kerry's forestry sites, and will thrive well in the ambient climate. Furthermore, these conifers mature in forty years; quality oak takes two hundred! Nonetheless, where soils permit, up to 10 per cent of new tree-planting is of

broadleaf varieties – rowan (*Sorbus*) and birch (*Betula*), which are included mainly for soil and habitat improvement.

But the most jolting facts which will emerge from any perusal of forestry statistics are these: Luxembourg has 31 per cent of land under forest; Ireland as a whole has 5 per cent; Kerry has 3.4 per cent!

There are also, of course, the older forests. The native oakwoods at Tomies Wood, Derrycunnihy Wood and Camillan Wood near Killarney, and Uragh Wood near Kenmare, are so old that they are worth many visits, and certain ancient individual trees – such as the 'Royal' oak, near Darby's Garden in Tomies Wood – are so vast in height and spread as to be quite breathtaking. Go and see for yourself what is stirring in the forests.

Fauna

Of Kerry's birds, the smallest breeding wisp of life – citizen of woodland, old and new – is the goldcrest (*Regulus regulus*). Even its orange-and-yellow crest does not detract from the effective grey-green camouflage, and in its busy lifestyle this 9cm midget does not sit around long enough for a second glance! Perhaps not even for a first!

Next time out, focus on something bigger – big and black and red-billed and red-legged and rare – the chough (*Pyrrhocorax pyrrhocorax*). Of only 656 breeding pairs of this highly aerobatic crow in Ireland, Kerry has two hundred, a number which, happily, has remained stable for some time in spite of the increased use of agricultural insecticides which tend to eliminate the chough's main food source. Cliff scenery, coastal rather than inland, is the normal habitat; perhaps this isolation is its salvation.

Then, you may say with a shrug, a tree-creeper is a tree-creeper, and a stonechat is a stonechat; they are both common enough wildbirds, one from the forest, and the other from the uncultivated heath-land outside it. But it is not as simple as that. Kerry boasts its own sub-species of tree-creeper (*Certhia familiaris*) and its own sub-species of

The gannet. These birds occupy every nook and cranny of Small Skellig.

stonechat (*Saxicola torquata*). Indeed, Kerry also boasts a sub-species of chaffinch (*Fringilla coelebs*), which is shared with county Limerick – but one begins to get lost in feather-splitting detail along this path.

It may be misleading – daunting too – to say that 380 species of wildbirds have been recorded in Ireland. Many would be migratory visitors, and unusual ones at that, but a more reasonable ambition would be to see perhaps half that number. For instance, in Killarney's 25,000 acre (10,300 hectare) National Park, 114 species of wildbirds have already been recorded. Of these sixty-four were resident, twelve were winter visitors and twenty were normal summer visitors. On the Kerry coast and islands, a further twenty-one breeding species are commonly found.

The future of that noisy summer visitor, the corncrake

(*Crex crex*), is in grave danger. Mechanical meadow-work in Ireland, apart from any foreign hazard during wintering in southern countries, is blamed for the great decline. Even in the 'good old days' it was generally impossible to catch sight of this furtive bird – slipping like a whisper through the tall meadow grass – but at least the unmistakable calling could be heard in every parish on every summer's evening. This is no longer the case. Leinster and central Munster are almost devoid of corncrakes. Kerry is one of its last outposts, and the few that are reported here are confined to the westernmost promontories, in the vicinity of Cahersiveen, Waterville, Valentia, Derrynane, Ballyferriter, Brandon, Castlegregory and Ballybunion. In all, less than fifty birds were recorded in a 1978 survey, and

61

since then the situation has unfortunately become worse.

Anyone who is lucky enough to hear a corncrake in future will be privileged indeed, and would do good work by reporting it to the Irish Wildbird Conservancy. If the day ever dawns when, like the corncrake, the human race itself is on the brink of extinction, it would be nice to think that someone, somewhere, gave a damn.

For anyone with a head for counting great numbers, Kerry's wetland habitats are exciting in winter — Castlemaine Harbour, Lough Gill (near Castlegregory), Tralee Bay, Barrow Harbour, Akeragh Lough and Lough Leane. Perhaps Castlemaine Harbour provides an adequate example. The following sightings were recorded in winter 1972-73: 1,460 mallard (*Anas platyrhynchos*); 2,000 teal (*Anas crecca*); 6,800 wigeon (*Anas penelope*); 2,000 pintail (*Anas acuta*); 900 shoveller (*Anas clypeata*); 4,200 brent geese (*Branta bernicla*); 2,350 oystercatcher (*Haematopus ostralegus*); 4,000 curlew (*Numenius arquata*); 3,000 bar-tailed godwit (*Limosa lapponica*); 300 redshank (*Tringa totanus*); 3,000 knot (*Calidris canutus*); 2,200 dunlin (*Calidris alpina*); and 3,000 golden plover (*Pluvialis apricaria*)!

SEABIRDS

In truth, it is the seabird colonies of the coast and estuaries that make the name of Kerry world-famous. The Kerry islands are spoken of with awe in this respect – not all of Kerry's fifty islands, of course, for some of them are too small to support even a rock pipit,

but rather the Skelligs, Puffin Island and the Blaskets group. Doulus Head – although it is part of the mainland – could also be included in this 'islands' category because its huge colonies of kittiwake (*Rissa tridactyla*), razorbill (*Alca torda*) and guillemot (*Uria aalge*) can be viewed only from the sea. Only a bird could land on the

The puffin has given its name to Puffin Island, home to thousands of the species.

Right: Coumeenole Beach near Slea Head, looking towards the Blasket Islands.

sheer ledges of Doulus Head, and even the wild goats that roam the area cannot approach them. (*See Islands section.*)

FISH

Coastal and lakeside fish life is in some danger when Kerry's seabirds drop in to dine! Nonetheless, two unusual fish species – as well as hoards of the

common species – survive in Kerry. A sub-species of char (*Savelinus alpinus fimbriatus*) lives in Coomasaharn Lake, near Glenbeigh, and in Killarney's lakes lives a peculiar land-locked variety of twaite shad (*Alosa fallax killarnensis*), a herring-like species which normally spends part of its life at sea, but in this case has

become a permanent resident in Killarney. Perhaps it is safer here. The Kerry coast, within striking distance of Small Skellig and its 23,000 pairs of gannet, is no place for a smart herring!

WHALE AND DOLPHIN

If it is not stretching territorial rights too much the whales which

show up in Kerry waters must surely be classed as exciting members of the Kerry fauna. It generally surprises many people to hear that whales occur in Ireland at all, but they do. It may be expecting too much to have a sighting every day, but at least three or four times in summer, usually July or August, some minke whales (*Balaenoptera acutorostrata*) are sighted within a couple of miles of land.

It is not obligatory to go by boat to look for them. Any prominent headland is worth a try. Brandon Point, frequently used as a birdwatching vantage point, would be just one example. Indeed, it was at Cloghane beach, quite near Brandon, on one sad occasion in November 1965 that some sixty-three pilot whales (*Globicephala melaena*) were stranded. At Ventry, on the other side of the Dingle Peninsula, in October 1967 five white-sided dolphins (*Lagenorhynchus acutus*) met a similar fate.

Summer 1985, for all its peculiar weather, was a particularly good year for sightings of the bottle-nosed dolphin (*Tursiops truncatus*), with many exciting experiences of large schools of them playing around fishing boats both near to and far off the coast. Anyone who has seen the dolphin's joyous aquabatics and the almost derisory ease with which they can 'make rings' around a speeding boat, will surely be convinced that these mammals have a capacity for a high intelligence worthy of much more of our attention.

Benign beings, all of them, with nothing but civility in their make-up, and the same could be said for the biggest fish of the area, the basking shark (*Cetorhinus maximus*), which cruises the Kerry coast in May and June and can be seen from many of the headland vantage points such as Slea Head. This creature is neither a man-eater nor even a mackerel-hunter, but supports its giant, ten-metre frame on a diet of plankton and such microscopic sea-dust. Little is known about the life of this huge fish, but, at least, the public outcry of some years ago banished the Norwegian harpoon-ships which hunted the basking shark mercilessly for its liver and fins, right up to the cliffs of Kerry.

SALMON

Next to Shark! Shark!, the word 'salmon' evokes the most reaction in Kerry, where a hotbed of vested interests crowds every side of every fence with views entrenched and irreconcilable about the salmon (*Salmo salar*). Basic to the chaos is a melee of hodge-podge, discriminatory legislation and a plethora of rights, customs and traditions going back to some dark ages, and now too hot, too confused and too involved for any authority to tackle seriously. For to tackle this salmon problem properly would be to wipe every current regulation off the statutes and begin anew.

Meanwhile, pending the arrival of that Utopian day, the Kerry salmon must run a gauntlet of deep-sea fishing trawlers in the maturing grounds off Iceland, a gauntlet of drift nets all along the west coast of Ireland, a gauntlet of weirs, traps and fixed nets in the home rivers, a gauntlet of effluent in some streams, of farmyard waste in others, finally to discover, after a two-year, two-thousand-mile trip, that the gravel of the native spawning beds has been dug up to make concrete blocks! And these are only the man-made hazards.

Amazingly, many salmon do survive and make it to Kerry's rivers, providing exciting sporting opportunities for a host of anglers who visit the area each year. There are some fifty rivers and at least thirty-six accessible lakes, where salmon, sea trout, or, indeed, small, sweet, brown trout, may be caught.

Waterville is the name most associated with the 'grand catch'. This village has dominated the Irish sea trout lists, sometimes, as in 1981, holding ten out of the fourteen Irish specimens, or, as in 1982, ten out of the twelve. But other places provide opportunities too — the 25.82lb (11.73kg) salmon landed at Killarney in February 1981 would be a good quarry for any encounter.

Successful sea-angling may be even easier to achieve, because a piece of string, a bent pin and a morsel left over from breakfast will be sure to catch *something!* But for those who aspire to greater conquests, Kerry's 250 miles (400km) of coastline has already provided specimens too numerous to mention, as well as a respectable proportion of the Irish records still standing in 1984:

Seals – if you are lucky you will see them congregate on the White Strand on Great Blasket, as you read about them in Tomás Ó Crohan's ' The Islandman'.

Conger eel (*Conger conger*): 72lb
    (32.72kg), Valentia, 1914

Red Sea-bream (*Pagellus bogaraveo*):
    9lb 6oz (4.26kg), Valentia, 1963

Sting ray (*Dasyatis pastinaca*): 51lb
    (23.18kg), Fenit, 1970

Undulate ray (*Raja undulata*): 18lb
    (8.18kg), Fenit, 1977

Ray's bream (*Brama brama*): 6lb
    4¼oz (2.85kg), Valentia, 1978

Monkfish (*Squatina squatina*): 73 lb
    (33.18kg) Fenit, 1980

Lesser spotted dogfish (*Scyliorhinus
    canicula*): 4¼lb (1.9kg), Valentia,
    1982

Greater spotted dogfish
    (*Scyliorhinus stellaris*): 23¾lb
    (10.79kg), Valentia, 1983.

SEALS

The seal lives a problematic and controversial existence on Kerry's coats. The grey seal (*Halichoerus grypus*) and the common seal (*Phoca vitulina*) are handy scapegoats for every wrong, real or imagined, and – although protected under the Wildlife Act – the seal, in the absence of any complete, up-to-date study, is guilty until proven innocent. The unlicensed poacher nets a salmon from the sea; the seal tears the salmon from the poacher's net; the poacher kills the seal, any seal. Some part of this strange equation is missing.

Who has not heard that old folktale which has long been a part of Kerry folklore and is found all along the west coast of Ireland, the west coast of Scotland, and even into Iceland? A fisherman is walking on the beach and he meets a brown-eyed girl resting on the rocks. He steals and hides her cloak to make her stay with him. They marry and have children — brown-eyed children. Years pass, and eventually one of the children finds the mother's old cloak and returns it to her, whereupon the mother slips away to the seashore and is seen no more.

A red deer stag – the mating call of the deer can be heard in the mountains near Killarney in October.

DEER

The Kerry deer may provide a rewarding day's hunting – strictly camera hunting – around Killarney. Dismiss the sika deer (*Cervus nippon*), they are latterday, Japanese blow-ins of 1861! Search for the true deer of Kerry, the red

Above: Windswept Lough Leane, looking towards Muckross, Killarney.

Right: Tralee Bay, with the Slieve Mish mountains in the background, taken from Blennerville.

deer (*Cervus elaphus*) – distinct from the sika, distinct from the fallow deer (*Dama dama*) of the Phoenix Park (Dublin), distinct even from the red deer of Donegal and Wicklow. Distinct in this important way: today's 350-strong red deer herd of Kerry is the only truly native herd in the country. They were roaming these wild mountains before humans ever set foot in Ireland. Indeed, it was probably the sheer vastness of their territory that saved them from extinction in the Famine years. To hear their bellows today, echoing around Torc and Mangerton mountains in the mating season of October leaves nobody in any doubt as to who is king of the Kerry wildlife today.

Kerry's last wolf was killed in 1710, and who else would dare challenge a red deer stag now? A pair of antlers of eight, ten or twelve points, mounted on an animal of 165 kilos, can make a convincing argument in any language! If prudence demands, it may be easier to view such a headdress mounted on a wall-plaque in the nearby folk museum at Muckross House.

THE KERRY COW

Those interested in farm animals, will discover something else of interest: not every cow in Kerry is a Kerry cow! In fact, very few are, for the 'Kerry' as a distinctive breed is now almost extinct. Allegedly descended from the ancient race of small cattle (*Bos longifrons*) which came to Ireland with the first farmers, the Kerry

breed was widespread in Ireland up to the seventeeth century. This was due, in great part, to the Kerry's unquestioned ability to thrive on sparse mountain pasture.

Even when imported breeds began to appear, the Kerry still retained its popularity in many of Kerry's large estates: James Butler, Waterville; Richard O'Mahony, Dromore Castle, Kenmare; Sir Maurice Fitzgerald, Knight of Kerry, Valentia; the Earl of Kenmare, Killarney; the Herbert Estate, Muckross. Even outside the county there were famous Kerry herds: the Earl of Clonmel, Straffan; the Earl of Rosse, Birr Castle; Viscount de Vesci, Abbeyleix; the Brabazon Hall Estate, England, and Harold Swithinbank, Denham Court, England.

Kerry cattle were first shown at the Royal Dublin Society in 1844;

a register of Kerry cattle was published in 1887; a *Kerry Herd Book* was issued in 1890. Today, a fine Kerry herd pays its way as a living, thriving, milking museum-piece at Muckross House. Kerry's Kerrys are really at home!

RARE SPECIES

If any corner of Kerry grips you, delve deeper. It may come as a piece of useless information that the only place in Ireland where you will find *Geomalacus maculosus* is in Kerry! *G. maculosus* is the greater spotted slug! Dark grey/green, spotted with white, and up to 9cm (3in) in length, its real home is Portugal or Spain, but it is alive and well and living in Killarney's Black Valley!

Similarly, those who search Ireland for *Bufo calamita* need look only in Kerry! *B. calamita* is the natterjack toad – the 'black frog', which runs rather than jumps, and is reported only at Castlemaine Harbour, Derrynane and Lough Gill (near Castlegregory).

And a sublime piece of apparently useless information is this: there may be less than ten insects per square foot in the county Antrim bogs, but there are 1,000 insects per square foot in the deciduous Kerry woodland! Luckily, not all of these are the biting, stinging, nuisance-making type, but are better renowned for their beauty or peculiar distribution. The brilliant purple of that oakwood denizen, the male purple hairstreak butterfly (*Thecla quercus*), is a joy to any eye. Two dragonflies, the downy emerald (*Cordulia aenea*) and the northern emerald (*Somatochlora arctica*), are, in Ireland, confined to Kerry, although they really belong to Scandinavia and the Alps. And, possibly the rarest creature of all – fortunately, because its name is almost unpronounceable – is a minute fly, known only to Kerry and two other places in the world. It is called *Buchonomyia thienemanni!*

These are the creatures, common and rare, that bring serious naturalists back to Kerry again and again, but you do not have to be a qualified specialist to appreciate the Kerry outdoors and its creatures great and small. A simple wildlife book will take you a long way, and the strange effect is this: once you stand in your favourite haunt – and this could be anywhere between Tarbert and Tooth mountain – even the roadside weeds will assume a special importance, almost a personal relationship, upon proper identification and recognition.

At least, in spite of Richard Hayward's outdated quip that ''tis a little aysht of north you'll go', there is no major language barrier in Kerry, except that the spoken English is about three times the tempo of that spoken in the Thames valley, or ten times that of Texas! Similarly, in *Gaeltacht* areas, the delivery of domestic dialogue is much too urgent for untuned ears. But once you can persuade Kerrymen to slow down their patter, in either language, you will encounter a fluency and richness of expression that is old and typical and unique.

Opposite: The Kerry cow, in Muckross National Park.

Left: The black-faced mountain sheep, with Inishtearacht in the background.

Above: A small lake near the Conor Pass, with Mount Brandon behind.

*Right: The golden tones of sunset over Smerwick Harbour, with
Great Blasket in the distance.*

A Love Affair

Kerry is like life. If you don't
experience it how can you know
what it is like? How can you
comment on it? A preconceived,
unproven notion is worthless. To
accept a stranger's version at face
value may be far from prudent.
Like life, Kerry takes time and it
may be a month, or perhaps a
year, before one can claim to have
an understanding, a special
partnership, even a full-blooded
love affair! But the relationship
must be a growing, maturing
agreement, with no preconditions
and no unreasonable expectations
Kerry, for its part, will not be
found wanting.

Index to Kerry placenames

Italics indicate reference to illustrations.

Select Bibliography

Barrington, T., *Discovering Kerry*, 1976; Corkery, D., *The Hidden Ireland*, 1924; MacAirt, S. (ed.), *The Annals of Inisfallen*, 1951; Mitchell, F., *The Irish Landscape*, 1976; O'Crohan, T., *The Islandman*, trans. Flower, R., 1937; O'Sullivan, M., *Twenty Years a-Growing*, trans. Davies, M.L. and Thomson, G., 1933; Pochin-Mould, D., *Valentia*, 1978; Praeger, R.L., *The Way that I Went*, 1937; Sayers, P., *An Old Woman's Reflections*, trans. Ennis, S., 1962; Scully, R.W., *Flora of County Kerry*, 1916; Synge, J.M., *In Wicklow and West Kerry*, 1912.